SEMINAR STUDIES IN HISTORY
General Editor: Roger Lockyer

The 1848 Revolutions

Peter Jones

Lecturer in History,
Charles Keene College
of Further Education,
Leicester

LONGMAN

LONGMAN GROUP UK LIMITED
Longman House, Burnt Mill, Harlow,
Essex CM20 2JE, England.
and Associated Companies throughout the world.

First published 1981
Fifth impression 1987
ISBN 0 582 35312 2

Set in 10/11 pt. Baskerville, Compugraphic

Produced by Longman Group (FE) Ltd
Printed in Hong Kong

British Library Cataloguing in Publication Data

Jones, Peter S.
   The 1848 revolutions — (Seminar studies in
   history).
   1. Europe — History — 1848–1849
   1. Title   II. Series
   940.2'84   D387

   ISBN 0–582–35312–2

Contents

Acknowledgements

We are grateful to the following for permission to reproduce copyright material:

Macmillan, London and Basingstoke for extracts from *Nations and Empires*: *Documents in the Political History of Europe and On Its Relations With the World Since 1648* by Bridges, Dukes, Hargreaves and Scott; Oxford University Press for an extract from a Nineteenth Century German publication, translated by G. A. Kertesz p. 125–6 of *Documents in the Political History of the European Continent 1815–1939*; Weidenfeld and Nicolson Ltd for extracts from *The Rise of the Working Class* by Jürgen Kuczynski.

The cartoon on the cover appeared in Punch in 1848.

Seminar Studies in History
Founding Editor: Patrick Richardson

Introduction

The Seminar Studies series was conceived by Patrick Richardson, whose experience of teaching history persuaded him of the need for something more substantial than a textbook chapter but less formidable than the specialised full-length academic work. He was also convinced that such studies, although limited in length, should provide an up-to-date and authoritative introduction to the topic under discussion as well as a selection of relevant documents and a comprehensive bibliography.

Patrick Richardson died in 1979, but by that time the Seminar Studies series was firmly established, and it continues to fulfil the role he intended for it. This book, like others in the series, is therefore a living tribute to a gifted and original teacher.

Note on the System of References:
A bold number in round brackets (**5**) in the text refers the reader to the corresponding entry in the Bibliography section at the end of the book. A bold number in square brackets, preceded by 'doc' [**docs 6, 8**] refers the reader to the corresponding items in the section of Documents, which follows the main text.

ROGER LOCKYER
General Editor

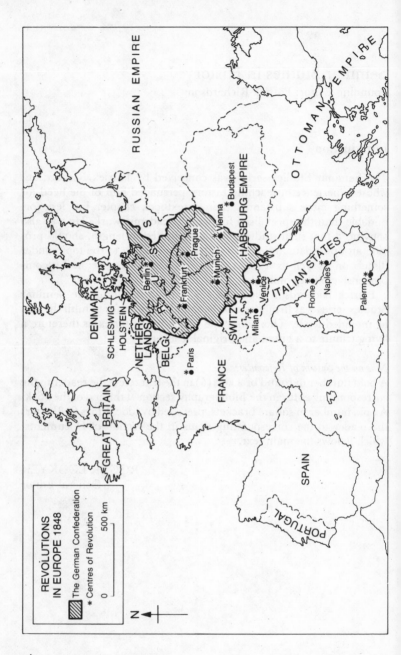

REVOLUTIONS
IN EUROPE 1848

▨ The German Confederation
* Centres of Revolution

0   500 km

N

RUSSIAN EMPIRE

OTTOMAN EMPIRE

HABSBURG EMPIRE

* Budapest
* Vienna
* Prague
PRUSSIA
* Berlin
* Frankfurt
* Munich
SWITZ.
* Milan
* Venice
ITALIAN STATES
* Rome
* Naples
* Palermo

DENMARK
SCHLESWIG
HOLSTEIN
NETHER-
LANDS
BELGIUM
GREAT BRITAIN
FRANCE
* Paris
SPAIN
PORTUGAL

Part One: The Background

1 The Outbreak of Revolution

On 20 February 1848 the reformers and the opposition to Guizot's government in France made plans to hold a political banquet in Paris. The banquet was banned by the government and, as a result, the common people of Paris held a procession through the streets in protest against this decision. Their leaders presented a petition to the Chamber of Deputies demanding Guizot's resignation.

The discontent against the government, and against Guizot in particular, had been growing during 1847 but then it had largely been a campaign of middle-class politicians. Now it was the cause of the common people of Paris and on 22 February 1848 the police had to clear an unruly crowd in the Place de la Madeleine. The next day the King, Louis Philippe, dismissed Guizot and called on Molé to lead the government. But this concession had come too late, because on the same evening a great throng of people had made their way along the Boulevard des Capucines to the Ministry of Foreign Affairs only to find their passage blocked by a troop of cavalry and infantry. According to Victor Hugo, the people at the head of the procession tried to stop and turn aside, 'but the irresistible pressure of the huge crowd weighed on the front ranks'. A shot rang out, and in the panic that followed a whole volley was fired. At least forty people were killed. The victims were piled on a cart lit with torches and within a few hours the city was blocked with barricades (**26**).

On the following morning, 24 February, Alexis de Tocqueville, a prominent member of the Chamber of Deputies, left his house feeling that he could 'scent revolution in the air'. A group of men gathered round him and asked for news, and he warned them that the only real danger to the government was if they themselves got too excited and took matters to extremes. ' "That's all very well, sir," they said, "the government has got itself into this fix by its own fault; so let it get itself out as best it can . . ." ' (**7**). Louis Philippe had done just that – he had abdicated that same afternoon and a Provisional Government had been set up.

The Provisional Government would probably have decided in favour of a Regency but the invasion of the Chamber of Deputies by a crowd of workers on the afternoon of 24 February pushed the Provisional Government towards a republic. Paris was now in the hands of the workers and the 'dangerous classes'. Earlier that day they had invaded the Tuileries Palace and dumped Louis Philippe's empty throne in the courtyard. According to Flaubert the 'common herd ironically wrapped themselves up in laces and cashmeres . . . Hats with ostrich feathers adorned blacksmiths' heads, and ribbons of the Legion of Honour supplied waistbands for the prostitutes' (quoted in **26**). Lamartine, who was popular with the people, nevertheless witnessed the invasion of the Chamber of Deputies with fear:

> They crowded the corridors, and rushed with their cries of mortal combat into the spectators' galleries. Their clothes torn, their shirts open, their arms bare, their fists clenched and resembling muscular clubs, their hair wildly dishevelled, and singed with cartridges, their countenances maddened with the delirium of revolution, their eyes smitten with the spectacle, so novel to them, presented by this Chamber . . . all revealed them as desperadoes, who were come to make the last assault on the last refuge of royalty (**57**).

They were armed with pikes, bayonets and sabres. 'Down with the Regency!' they shouted, 'The Republic forever'. Their demonstration meant that the new Provisional Government was forced to include the socialists Louis Blanc and Flocon, as well as a solitary but symbolic worker, Albert.

The revolution in France was followed by outbreaks of violence and revolutionary activity in southern Germany, where the peasants of the Odenwald and Schwarzwald descended on their landlords' castles and destroyed the charters which perpetuated their feudal obligations. In Bavaria the revolution was intertwined with an old-style court scandal: King Ludwig's infatuation with the dark-eyed beauty, Lola Montez, had led him to consult her on political matters. He made her Countess of Landsberg, despite protests from ministers, the clergy and even the Pope. Her arrogance and insulting behaviour so incensed the students at the University of Munich that they launched an attack on her house in February 1848. The King attempted to have the university closed, but the news of the abdication of Louis Philippe brought crowds on to the streets calling for a republic. Ludwig was forced to banish his beloved Lola and soon abdicated, leaving the throne to his son Maximilian. But it was not just the opposition in the streets that had forced Ludwig's hand: it was also the dissatisfaction among the business and professional classes who demanded a more liberal régime.

By March the revolutions had spread eastwards to Berlin, the capital of Prussia, and to Vienna, Prague and Budapest. Traditionally it has been claimed that the French example was enough to spark off revolution throughout Europe, but events elsewhere had already taken on dangerous proportions. The potato crop in 1846 and 1847 had been destroyed by disease, causing food riots among the poorer classes in much of central Europe. Early in January 1848 there had been riots in Milan and this had culminated in the famous 'five days' street fighting in March, where the Italians had succeeded in expelling the Austrian garrison. January had also seen an insurrection in Palermo, in Sicily.

The Revolutions of 1848 had two important features. First, they were widespread – there were even revolutions in Pernambuco in South America and later in Colombia. Secondly, they seemed initially successful. In Prussia King Frederick William IV temporarily went with the revolution, parading the streets swathed in the German national flag. But the most startling victory of the revolutionary year was the resignation of Metternich, not only the principal architect of the Settlement of 1815, but for many the symbol of order and stability in Europe. Troubles in Vienna had grown from the moment that the news of the revolution in Paris had arrived. On 13 March the Diet of Lower Austria, a traditional assembly that contained some liberal-minded aristocrats, was invaded by a crowd of workers and students. Metternich agreed, along with Windischgrätz, the Provincial Governor of Bohemia, that swift action would quell the uprising. But it was too late. Metternich had lost the support of the Court and was soon to lose the ability to take the decisive action that he claimed was necessary. So it was against a background of popular revolution in the streets that Metternich resigned and eventually made his way to England as an exile.

The great Habsburg Empire, which Metternich had so long maintained, seemed on the point of disintegration: the Italians of Lombardy and Venetia were seeking to break free from the grip of Vienna; the Hungarians led by Kossuth were staking their claim for independence; and the first rumblings of Czech nationalism were making themselves heard in Prague. All this vigorous activity was not caused by the example of the French alone even though Michelet's claim of 1846 may seem prophetic: 'France possesses the divine genius of society . . . she is the pilot of the ship of humanity' (quoted in **16**). The outbreak of revolution in those places already mentioned, as well as in Venice, Rome, Naples, Frankfurt and many of the smaller German states, together with troubles in Ireland and Britain, had general causes to be found in the years before 1848. Perhaps, because most of the revolutions took place in the major cities, the historian can find the clues to some more general causes and explanations that go beyond a slavish imitation of the French example. Of course there were particular causes in different countries but there were nevertheless general European explanations which arose out of the general nature of European society. It will be necessary to examine these causes in turn.

Part Two: The European Transformation

From the beginning of the eighteenth century Europe had undergone a significant transformation. There were two major elements in this: the first was the onset of industrialisation and the growth of towns, particularly in England, but later in France and Germany; the second was the growth of population in the countryside, which placed great strain on the resources of survival of the poorer sections of the rural population. These two major social and economic developments set into motion the long-term strains that helped to bring about the revolutions of 1848, which themselves marked the climax to a revolutionary period that had begun in France in 1789.

2   The Impact of Industrialisation on the Working Classes

European writers in the 1830s and 1840s were impressed primarily by the growth of industrial power within their society. The problems of the countryside probably seemed less immediate to them. Nonetheless, the strains of population pressure that were felt in the countryside should not be ignored by the historian as it is often less obvious factors that are the springs of great events like revolutions. Contemporary writings, however, show that it was with the pathological problems of urban living – disease, mortality and overcrowding – that educated society was most concerned. In England these writings formed part of a debate on the 'Condition of England' question. Similar debates were carried on among the respectable classes of many European cities. The great fear of the respectable classes was of the urban poor who had already shown their dangerous potential in Paris in 1789 and continued to exhibit, apparently, the depravities of drunkenness, criminality and begging (*52*). What, then, was the real extent of the problem?

In France the most significant industrial region was in the north-east of the country, based on the towns of Roubaix and Lille. The pace of industrialisation in France was much slower than that in Britain. Nonetheless France was probably the most industrially advanced state on the continent of Europe in 1848. Much of France's industrial development was not technologically advanced – for example, in the 1840s only forty-one blast furnaces out of a total of 462 used coke (the remainder used charcoal). But there was considerable development of metallurgical industries, and in 1848 there were some 3,220 kilometres of railway. This railway building was backed by government investment and this fact is pertinent to the causes of the 1848 revolutions in France (see below, p. 30).

Even though the speed of French industrialisation was slower than the British, the new industrial towns exhibited just the same lurid features as the industrial and commercial cities of Leeds and Manchester. In 1848 there were some 400,000 factory workers in France. The growth of factory production disrupted the traditional world of the artisan whose guild associations broke down: they were now faced with competition for jobs from immigrant labour from the countryside. Many of the newcomers were uneducated and in Mulhouse in the 1840s it has been estimated that almost three-quarters of the illiterates were born outside the city. These new factory workers were often rootless, showing their discontent by resorting to drink, abandoning religious practice, and by stealing, especially from their place of work (*33*, *76*). Clearly such behaviour indicates a breakdown of the normal controls that had prevailed in the more traditional society of the countryside. Some historians have equated a rise in criminality and social disaffection with an increase in revolutionary and protest activity (*76*). It is certainly true that the revolution in France and elsewhere came at the end of a long period of strikes and local rebellions, including bread riots in Lille in 1830 and 1847, and in Mulhouse in 1847.

There is no doubt that the condition of the industrial worker of France was grim. He could expect to die sooner than an agricultural worker, although in Lille the expectation of life of a worker rose from twenty-eight years to thirty-two in the period 1830 to 1848. His diet was extremely monotonous and even the better paid 'spent at least half their income on starches alone' (*33*). But there is no real evidence to suggest that the process of industrialisation in France significantly depressed working-class standards of living in quantitative terms. For example, the total meat consumption per capita 'appears to have remained unchanged from 1812 to 1840' (**21**). Yet, although the standard of living of the French worker was probably slightly better than his German counterpart (he was less dependent on the potato), his way of life was often wretched: the working day in France was often fourteen or fifteen hours compared with about thirteen hours in Germany (**23**). The living conditions of the French worker were exceptionally squalid and he was of course vulnerable to disease. The cholera epidemic of 1831–32 carried off 18,400 people in Paris alone in a span of six months.

Despite industrialisation, the traditional artisan continued to form a distinct section of society, particularly in France and Germany, and this group had the largest claims to organisation and to some group identity. The wellbeing and status of the artisans, as has already been indicated, was severely undermined by industrialisation, and their traditional guilds had been made illegal by law. Nonetheless, they were quick to form new organisations and some of them became attracted by the new ideology of socialism. It was clear that some of the workers in the Lyons insurrection of 1834 had become aware of the writings of Babeuf, Blanqui, Blanc and Proudhon. During the insurrection the silk weavers stressed the need for the equal distribution of wealth and 'addressed their remarks to one specific class, the workers; and this, in itself, was new' (**32**). It was also in the 1830s that the secret societies and political clubs again became active. Of particular importance was Blanqui's Societies of the Families and the Society of the Rights of Man. These groups were to play a lively part in the events of 1848. Thus, where the disruption of traditional artisan life was accompanied with the growth of new forms of working-class organisation and the development of new political beliefs such as socialism, all the ingredients of a powerful revolutionary recipe were present.

The degree of worker organisation, however, varied from one part of Europe to another. It was in Britain that the workers were most effectively organised, but even they could not wield power at a national level, even though they attempted to do so through Chartism in the late 1830s and early 1840s. Chartism proved remarkably ineffective in 1848.

In Germany the great regional variation of industrial development meant that there were no integrated national organisations. The number of industrial enterprises in Germany before 1848 was very small, and even later giants like Krupp only employed 150 workers in 1846. In 1849 there were only thirty-two out of a total of 247 blast furnaces in Prussia operating by coke. Railway development, too, was still slow, so that there were only 549 kilometres of railway in the German states in 1840. But like the government of Louis Philippe in France, the Prussian government of Frederick William IV also became embroiled in the problems of railway investment. This may have been a significant reason for Frederick William IV's tinkering with liberal reform, which was at least one of the more immediate factors in the causes of the Revolution of 1848 in Prussia. Railway building in Prussia and in the other German states had been progressing at a considerable pace since the first line had been opened in Bavaria in 1835. Difficulties with raising capital in the early 1840s had led the Prussian government to invest in railways and also to make guarantees to private companies. Despite the backing of the state no private company had undertaken to build a railway from Berlin to East Prussia, the heartland of *Junker* wealth. Not surprisingly, the *Junkers* themselves began pressing Frederick William IV to give state backing for the building of an *Ostbahn* (Eastern Railway). Such an undertaking would have required a considerable increase in taxation, and not even Prussian absolutism felt strong enough to raise taxation of this order without some representative or constitutional backing. In 1820 the previous king, Frederick William III, had promised that any increase in the state debt would not be taken on without the approval of some representative body. Consequently, in 1847 Frederick William IV called a United Diet. Apart from representatives from the aristocracy there were also bankers, merchants, professional men and provincial mayors. The United Diet put forward a set of classical liberal demands including regular meetings and more stringent control over taxation. The King refused; and in return the Diet refused to approve the raising of a state loan of thirty million *thalers*. The situation was deadlocked and the Diet subsequently broke up, but the experience was not lost on the *Junkers* or on the King. Prussian absolutism had faced a severe setback in the year before the revolutions. Apparently Prussian liberalism, as shown by the stubborn resistance of the United Diet to the demand for a loan for the *Ostbahn*, was a force to be reckoned with. The confidence of the monarchy had certainly been shaken. It may have been this fact that led to Frederick William IV's early capitulation to liberal demands in 1848.

Apart from the political implications of railway building, industrialisation in Prussia and the other German states had severe social implications, even though industrial development east of the Rhine was not as great as that in Britain, or even in France. It was not necessarily the extent of industrialisation as measured in crude statistical terms – kilometres of railways and output of coal and iron – that brought about revolution. More likely was the change from one type of socio-economic organisation to another: the replacement of feudalism by capitalism.

The change from feudalism to capitalism or private enterprise in Prussia was very rapid. After the Prussian defeat by the French at the Battle of Jena in 1806 the Prussian state began vigorously to overhaul and reform many of its institutions. This included the abolition of hereditary serfdom. There is no doubt that the rapid development of modern industry in Germany was especially painful for the worker. Undoubtedly, his standard of living declined, particularly in the 1840s. In 1844 the per capita meat consumption was 87.6 lbs (39.7 kg) in the German states; by 1847 this had fallen to 77 lbs (34.9 kg) per capita. In Munich the average meat consumption was 245 lbs (111.1 kg) per capita in the period 1809–19. By 1839–49 this had fallen to 188 lbs (85.3 kg) [**docs 3a–e**]. There were similar falls in Hamburg and Lubeck. At the same time people appeared to be drinking more. The same problems were apparent outside Germany and were reflected by the upsurge of a lively temperance agitation. But ultimately the change from agrarian feudalism to industrial capitalism in the German states and in other parts of central Europe led to a weakening of traditional forms of authority and control. This exhibited itself in an increase in riots and strikes and eventually the formation by German workers of an Industrial Code.

The formulation of a set of demands specifically in the working-class interest leads into a particularly controversial area of political and historical debate – the question of a special 'class consciousness'. This is a very complex subject and a full analysis would be inappropriate here. It is nevertheless important to indicate at least some of the ideas involved. 'Class consciousness' is a term of special relevance to Marxist historians because, for Marx, historical change grew out of conflicts between classes or economic interests. Of great importance to Marx therefore was the economic organisation of society, since changes in the system of economic organisation or the mode of production lead to changes in the social organisation. A new language became necessary to describe society. Before industrialisation commentators spoke of 'ranks', 'degrees' or 'interests' when describing social difference. The term 'working-class' first appeared in English writing shortly after 1815; in France the term did not come into popular usage until after 1830. Marx argued that as industrialisation developed so each class evolved its own consciousness. For the middle classes, or bourgeoisie, as Marx called them, the fact that they controlled or owned the forces of production meant that they developed a special belief in freedom of opinion and liberalism generally, as well as more specifically a belief in freedom of enterprise. Working-class consciousness involved a realisation of the fact that the middle class owned the means of production. It was this realisation that led the working class to the belief in the necessity of a revolutionary social-ism. This was the special 'working-class consciousness'. Thus the working-class 'consciousness' was distinct from the bourgeois 'con-sciousness'. Marx would have regarded the latter as reforming rather than revolutionary.

The question of class consciousness is very important to the study of the causes of the 1848 revolutions. Did those who took to the streets and lost their lives have a 'consciousness' of their place within so-ciety? The question is probably unanswerable in any obvious or cat-egorical sense. It is, however, necessary for the historian to consider whether the transformation of Europe from one type of economic sys-tem to another – from feudalism to capitalism – produced a belief among working people of the necessity of revolution as the sole solu-tion to their grievances. For some historians there is no doubt that the 1848 revolutions were made by the working class, since it was the workers who died on the barricades and fought on the streets. 'It was their hunger that powered the demonstrations that turned into revolutions' (**20**).

Death in a revolutionary uprising does not necessarily tell us much about the identity of interest that is a precondition of class conscious-ness. In England, it has been argued that a working-class conscious-ness emerged out of the struggle for the Reform Bill between 1830 and 1832 (**38**). This view has been refined to take into account local variations. The presence of a resident capitalist class or bourgeoisie, it has been suggested, which financed local industry, intensified the sense of working-class consciousness in Oldham (**19**). That is because the working class could clearly identify the class who were 'exploiting' them in Marx's definition of the word. This class consciousness re-sulted in the erosion of the separate sectional interests of skilled and unskilled workers – a process which has been measured in Oldham by the high level of intermarriage between these two sectional in-terests. There was thus a general collective interest that cut across the separate interests of skill and status. In other towns in England, such as Northampton where the shoe industry was financed from London, the absence of a resident capitalist class meant that the development of working-class consciousness was weak or retarded (**19**).

This same pattern may apply to the Continent. For example, the fact that much of the industry of northern Italy was financed from Switzerland and Germany (14) may have meant that Italian workers showed little consciousness of the nature of their exploitation. In the uprising led by Daniel Manin in Venice in 1848, only a demand for the abolition of the salt tax emerged as a specific demand of the workers. In France and Germany the working class exhibited a much stronger sense of identity or 'consciousness' by formulating demands that were reckoned to ameliorate their condition as workers. It may be, then, that the 1848 revolutions were caused in part by the effect of industrialisation on the working class, in that the latter assumed a more precise awareness of their place within a society that was moving in the direction of industrial capitalism.

The repression of working-class organisations in the post-revolutionary June Days in France and the October Days in Vienna showed clearly the division of interests between the propertied and the non-propertied classes: 1848 drew the lines of definition. The working-class insurrections failed; the middle-class revolutions had qualified success. After the revolutions the middle classes were able to accelerate the process of industrial expansion, especially in the authoritarian Second Empire and behind the safe confines of the Zollverein in Germany.

So industrialisation disrupted the traditional life of the artisan in major cities like Paris. At the same time the rural labourers who were forced off the land for one reason or another were unable to reconcile themselves to their new environment (76). Consequently any major disaster, such as a food shortage, was likely to produce a violent response. Moreover, industrialisation may have produced a special working-class 'consciousness' that was potentially revolutionary. This 'consciousness' may have manifested itself in 1848 [**doc. 3e**].

3 The Impact of Industrialisation on the Middle Classes

For some historians the rise of the middle class – in terms of economic and political power – is the outstanding feature of the process of European industrialisation in the nineteenth century. (**29**). The revolutions of 1848 are certainly a landmark in this process. But what exactly do historians mean when they talk of the 'middle class' in the nineteenth century? In Western Europe the middle class can be divided into three major interest groups. Firstly, there was the upper middle class of manufacturers, bankers and merchants. In France this group was collectively known as the *grande bourgeoisie*; this was an extremely small section of French society, but one which wielded considerable power, especially in the reign of Louis Philippe. This political power stemmed from its economic strength. For instance, in Paris in the period 1830 to 1848 one per cent of the middle class controlled 30 per cent of the wealth of the whole of the group termed middle-class. Similar concentrations of wealth existed elsewhere: in Berlin in 1848 there were only 712 merchants of any note out of a total population of 400,000 (**48**).

The *grande bourgeoisie* of France was generally very conservative in outlook, often aspiring to the way of life of the aristocracy. It has been observed, in fact, that the bourgeoisie of Paris preferred to invest in land rather than further their industrial enterprises. In 1820, 36.5 per cent of the Departmental electors were described in the tax returns as *professions économiques* (businessmen), whereas 46.2 per cent were described as *propriétaires* (property owners). This latter group presumably enjoyed a private income that enabled its members to lead the grand life in imitation of the aristocracy of the *ancien régime*. By 1842 only 29.4 per cent of the electors could be described as businessmen, whereas 49.9 per cent could be described as *propriétaires* or without profession (**68**). Clearly the *grande bourgeoisie* aspired to the status of aristocrats. There was certainly a security in landownership that was probably less risky than industrial enterprise. The *grande bourgeoisie* was not then a revolutionary class or even a class that sought extensive reform. Its complacency and confidence may have taken a jolt, however, in the financial crisis of 1846–47, turning it against the government of Louis Philippe.

Next in status to the upper middle class of businessmen and manufacturers were the professionals: lawyers, doctors, teachers and customs officials. In western Europe this group probably represented as much as 10 per cent of the whole of the middle class (*33*). The professional classes developed with the growth of state bureaucracy and the associated increase in higher education that was essential to the training of state officials (*49*). In France, attendance at *lycées* doubled between 1809 and 1842. Not all the men who benefited from higher education found a place in the state bureaucracy: many entered the 'free professions' of law and medicine. There were many whose ambition for public office went unsatisfied. Competition for office at local and national level was , in fact, one of the major conflicts of the so-called 'Bourgeois Monarchy'. Like most labels the term 'Bourgeois Monarchy' was not entirely accurate, as it was really the *grande bourgeoisie* who were the force behind Louis Philippe's régime. It was the *grande bourgeoisie*, together with the landed notables, who composed the voting class in the 'Bourgeois Monarchy'. Many professional men were not sufficiently wealthy to qualify for the vote during Louis Philippe's reign, even though the electorate increased from 160,000 in 1830 to 240,000 by 1846 (*53*). Guizot, the dominant politician of the 'Bourgeois Monarchy', argued that this natural increase would continue as the country grew more wealthy (*39*). Presumably, all sections of society would in time qualify for the vote, according to Guizot's argument. In the meantime many educated men were extremely dissatisfied and became increasingly critical of Guizot's government in the 1840s.

The problem of the imbalance between the number of educated men and the number of opportunities for state office was even more acute in the German and Italian states than it was in France. In Prussia the civil service was dominated by the aristocracy as it was in many of the smaller states. An education in law was an essential prerequisite of a state post in Prussia, and the number of law students increased by almost a third in the decade after 1841. To compensate for this overproduction of law students, the state introduced a more rigorous entrance examination for the civil service with the result that a 25 per cent failure rate was achieved. Further, those that passed the examination had to serve an arduous apprenticeship, during which they received no pay. In 1848 there were 4,000 apprentices in the system. Between 1836 and 1848 the judicial branch offered about twenty positions a year, and ten apprentices died annually while waiting. Those who escaped death were required to maintain an expensive front and their general behaviour was kept under close watch by the police (**33**, **49**), [**doc. 1b**].

The educated classes in France, Germany and Italy were probably the most dissatisfied section of the middle class as a whole. Given the part played by educated men in 1848, particularly in the German Assemblies (**18**, **77**, **81**), their career problems and general frustration of opportunity may have been decisive in pushing them towards agitation (**49**). Even as early as 1820 Metternich had observed that the 'agitated classes' were for the most part the educated [**doc. 1b**]. This view was clear in his action in 1819, when he forced upon the German states the Carlsbad Decrees by which he hoped to suppress liberal ideas within the universities [**doc. 1c**].

After the *grande bourgeoisie* and the professional classes, the third group to be considered within the general bracket of the middle class is the lower middle class, principally the shopkeepers and small employers. The shopkeepers were not an especially wealthy class, and in France they may have been drawn towards republicanism in the 1840s. They were not usually rich enough to qualify for the 200 franc franchise of 1830, and they certainly became critical of Guizot's rule. It is worth remembering that, although the June Days Revolution of 1848 was dominated by artisans, there were 119 jewellers and 191 wine merchants arrested out of a total of 11,693 arrests (**32**).

The pattern then is clear: nineteenth-century Europe was marked by the rise of the middle class. The businessmen and manufacturers were the first to make inroads into regions previously controlled by the privileged aristocracy. In France the position of the *grande bourgeoisie* was sufficiently secure to make them agents of social and political conservatism. In Germany and Italy the business classes were not revolutionary, but they may have realised the economic value of nationalism. The other sections of the middle class were hardly so successful before 1848, and it was this lack of success that pushed the educated classes and the lower middle-class shopkeepers and small employers into demanding more far-reaching changes in the systems of government which they encountered.

4 Population Pressure and the Condition of Agricultural Society

The changes that have been outlined so far were changes that primarily affected urban life. In order to understand the causes of the 1848 revolutions more fully it is necessary to appreciate the great pressure that was placed on the agricultural system from the middle of the eighteenth century to the middle of the nineteenth century. Crudely put this was a matter of numbers. In the middle of the eighteenth century the population of Europe was between 120 and 140 million; by 1800 this had risen to 187 million and by 1840 to 266 million. This growth was not entirely due to urban development. In Germany some rural areas showed a more dramatic population growth than urban areas. For example, in the substantially rural areas of Pomerania, in eastern Prussia, the population increased from 683,000 in 1816 to 1,198,000 in 1849 – a 75 per cent increase. The population of the industrial region of Arnsberg-Dusseldorf on the other hand grew from 968,000 in 1816 to 1,198,000 in 1849 – only a 54 per cent increase. More significantly, perhaps, for the 1848 revolutions, the Pomeranian population increased by 1.41 per cent per annum between 1840 and 1849, whereas the population of Arnsberg-Dusseldorf increased by 1.18 per cent per annum in the same period (**40**). Such a rate of growth put great pressure on food supplies, and it is reasonably safe to say that by 1840 many parts of Europe were overpopulated, in that food supply was insufficient and there was considerable unemployment.

Population pressure naturally caused migration. Many people emigrated beyond Europe, but there were extensive movements within Europe itself. There was a considerable movement of population from the Low Countries into north-eastern France in the 1840s, and from the German states there were 54,000 emigrants in the period 1841–45 and 182,000 in 1846–50 (**43**). Clearly the rate of migration from the German states was considerably greater in the years most immediate to the revolutions. It is fairly certain that these population movements were a symptom of food shortages that were most acutely felt in the late 1840s.

Apart from food shortages and land hunger generally, the Euro-

15

pean population was also subject to intermittent decimation from the predatory cholera. In France, there were probably 100,000 deaths attributable to the epidemic of 1836–37, compared with some 50,000 deaths in Britain. There were further outbreaks in 1847–49 and again in 1851–54. Clearly, too, a large portion of the European population was extremely vulnerable to natural disasters whether from famine, the less extreme fluctuations of food prices [**doc. 4**], or the more definite possibility of death from disease. Such a vulnerable population was always potentially violent. This potential was realised in 1848.

There were also changes that affected the class relations of those who lived on the land. At the beginning of the nineteenth century aristocrats still held important political positions in most European states. In Britain the aristocratic control over government was such that between 1832 and 1866 only twelve ministers in the cabinet were lawyers and only five were businessmen, whereas sixty-four were from aristocratic families. Elsewhere in Europe the aristocracy formed the core of the political class and dominated positions in the state bureaucracy, the Church and the army. Only in France, where the Revolution of 1789 had adulterated the pure *noblesse*, could it be said that the traditional aristocracy had been decisively excluded from power. In central and eastern Europe the nobility still exercised considerable control through the provincial diets, where they had control over taxation and administration. In Prussia 9 out of 11 ministers, 29 out of 30 diplomats, 20 out of 28 provincial governors and 7,264 out of 9,434 army officers were *Junkers* (**34**). Aristocratic honour in Prussia was also given legal recognition: an aristocrat's word in a court of law was accepted without an affidavit. Of course such privileges were closely guarded by the aristocracy, and it was their actions and fears that determined the nature of political rule between 1815 and 1848; in the long run, therefore, these actions were important causes of the revolutions of 1848.

. The political power of the aristocracy was derived from land. Land was the great measure of wealth. In Britain 500 members of the peerage owned half the total acreage at the beginning of the nineteenth century. In Prussia, east of the Elbe, it was the *Junkers* who dominated; in Silesia alone half the total acreage was owned by fifty-four families. In the Habsburg lands the concentration of landownership was unparalleled except in Russia, and in the province of Hungary the number of truly large landowners or 'magnates' did not exceed 200 families (**26**).

This highly concentrated pattern of landownership did not apply in France; nonetheless landownership was still a mark of status [**doc. 6**].

Thus, although the revolution of 1789 had broken up the large estates, the ownership of land, no matter how little, was a badge of social distinction. In 1789 there were 400,000 landowning aristocrats in France; by 1800 there were about six million small landowners. Admittedly there remained some large estates of between 200 and 400 hectares notably in western France, and the owners of these lands, the provincial notables, still retained much of their political power even in the period 1830 to 1848.

In addition to controlling wide expanses of land the European aristocracy also controlled the lives of vast sections of humanity itself, principally the peasantry. The condition of the peasantry was one of the most important underlying factors affecting the stability of European civilisation. The peasantry often proved volatile, and their participation in the French Revolution of 1789 was well recognised by the owners of property. In central and eastern Europe there were several examples of peasant disorder, especially in the 1840s. For instance there was the revolt of the Silesian weavers in 1844, and in the Habsburg lands there was an uprising of Polish nobles in the province of Galicia in 1846. Metternich's appeal to the peasantry to put down the rising was a successful but two-edged sword. The viciousness with which the Polish peasants attacked their Polish masters was watched with trepidation by all landowners, irrespective of their nationality.

The potential violence of the peasantry may well be explained by their wretchedness. Some 70 per cent of the peasantry's income was spent on food (33). Therefore, any rapid increase in the price of bread or potatoes was bound to bring the most extreme hardship. Consequently the failure of the 1846 harvest and the poor harvest that followed should not merely be regarded as a short-term cause of revolution. The possibility of harvest failure was inherent in the European system of agriculture. The consequences of such a failure had been made worse by the unprecedented increase in the European population that had begun in the eighteenth century.

In addition to the basic problem of a potential massive food shortage, the condition of the European peasantry was also being affected by a change in the system of economic organisation. Thus, although I have used the term peasantry to describe all those who worked directly on the land, the peasantry was not really a homogeneous group. For instance, the peasantry of France was a class of independent small holders. In England it is not strictly correct to talk of a peasantry at all, for the effects of enclosure had transformed the peasantry into a class of landless agricultural wage-labourers. In eastern Europe, on the other hand, something like a traditional peasantry remained. Peasants were expected to perform the feudal 'labour service' for their masters. Admittedly there were many regional variations, although it can generally be accepted that the degree of servility increased on moving eastwards in Europe (**21**). In central Europe – the German states and the Italian peninsula – the two types of economic system co-existed. Reforms in Prussia in the early nineteenth century had led to the dismantling of much of the feudal system. Elsewhere, especially in the Habsburg lands, many of the feudal taxes and dues, such as the *robot* or labour rent, remained. Thus in addition to food shortages it should also be appreciated that the system of agricultural production was often a source of grievance. These grievances became prominent in 1848.

5 The Breakdown of Traditional Political Control

Just as the forces of economic and social change disrupted the traditional world of the artisan in the cities and the life of the peasant in the countryside, so they also affected the official institutions of the state. Until the French Revolution of 1789 the rule of kings had not been seriously questioned on the continent of Europe. After the defeat of Napoleon there was a general determination on the part of the European aristocracy and the statesmen who met at Vienna in 1815 to restore the power of monarchy and therefore general political stability. The Vienna Settlement was more then than just a set of territorial arrangements between the major powers of Europe; it was also a general political settlement that aimed to bring about the reassertion of the ideas of the *ancien régime* – legitimate monarchy, the power of the Church and the power of rank and aristocratic privilege [**doc. 1a**].

In the decade after 1815 European statesmen strove to maintain these principles against the insidious threat of radical jacobinism, nationalism and even limited constitutional government. Metternich's Carlsbad Decrees of September 1819 [**doc. 1c**] had their equivalent in the repressive Six Acts passed in Britain in the same year. Metternich had good cause to be concerned, as the years immediately after 1815 were punctuated by a number of revolutionary outbreaks principally in Spain, Naples and Greece. The political reaction that followed these revolutions was generally severe – in Naples the King appointed a Minister of Vengeance to wage a counter-revolution (**94**). The spectre of revolution was always in the forefront of the minds of the kings and ruling statesmen of Europe from 1815 to 1848; and it was this fear of revolution that often determined the decision of the kings and their advisors.

The danger of revolution was highly developed in the mind of Metternich, although the actual possibility of revolution was probably most real in France. The statesmen at Vienna had worked to provide stability in France by restoring the Bourbon monarchy in the person of Louis XVIII. Further, the excessive power of the French king, which had been one of the major causes of grievance in 1789, was to be curtailed by a constitution that was to possess a representative element in the form of a Chamber of Deputies. The power of the king was however still considerable [**doc. 1d, e**], although the French monarchy was less autocratic than some of its European counterparts. It was still predisposed to the old habits of patronage, favouritism and court intrigue. Louis XVIII's infatuation for Mme du Cayla, with whom he played chess, led to the improved political fortunes of Villèle, who became President of the Council in 1822. Villèle was apparently ghost writer for Mme du Cayla's daily letter to the King (*53*).

The experiment of Constitutional Monarchy under the patronage of the Bourbons ultimately failed in the hands of Charles X, the brother of Louis XVIII. The production of the Ordinances of St Cloud in 1830 brought about the revolution of that year [**doc. 1d**]. Monarchy, however, still survived in the form of Louis Philippe, the former duc d'Orléans. Metternich's fears were justified, as the revolution which brought down Charles X produced revolutionary shock waves throughout the rest of Europe, leading to the first revision of the Vienna Settlement and the establishment of the independent kingdom of Belgium. There is no doubt that after the 1830 revolutions the European monarchs had to be more watchful, and none more so than Louis Philippe, whose government had to suppress a major insurrection at Lyons in 1834.

Theoretically the government of Louis Philippe was constitutional, in that his power was restrained by representative institutions. In practice considerable power still lay with the king, and like Louis XVIII and Charles X, Louis Philippe had the power personally to initiate legislation. Understandably, therefore, there was always the possibility of a conflict between the Chamber of Deputies and the King, since the Chamber was expected to debate and approve legislation proposed by the King [**doc. 1e**]. The conflict between the King's minister, Guizot, and the Chamber of Deputies became the most prominent political feature of the government of the July Monarchy in the 1840s.

Other Europeans regarded France as an essentially liberal state. East of the Rhine Europe was made up of a multitude of non-constitutional states where the kings and princes felt no need to justify their authority. For instance, with the restoration of the House of Savoy in the Kingdom of Piedmont-Sardinia in 1815, the new King Victor Emmanuel I threw the whole state into chaos with a solitary edict by refusing to recognise any law passed since 1777. The aristocracy again became exempt from taxation and the Church regained its ancient rights (*94*). Autocracy in the Habsburg Empire was equally vigorous and has been aptly called a 'monarchical machine' (*88*). The fear of concessions to any form of liberal constitutionalism was acutely felt by Metternich and in January 1848 he wrote: 'The impending conflict will tear the mask from the face of reform to show it in all its horror as the spectre of radicalism' (**17**). Thus for Metternich liberal constitutional reform was a Trojan horse that would eventually bring down all the established institutions of the state.

Living in fear of revolution meant that state policies were highly repressive. Karl Marx wrote scathingly of the Habsburg Empire under Metternich: 'All around the frontier wherever the Austrian States touched upon a civilised country a cordon of literary censors was established.' Western liberal historians have tended to assume that such repression was in itself a cause of radical and even revolutionary activity. For instance, A. J. P. Taylor, writing about the Habsburg Empire, says: 'Though foreign books and papers were forbidden, the educated classes knew what was astir in the world, and, long before 1848, there was a clear radical programme, not on paper but in men's minds' (**88**). It may be, however, that the repression in the Habsburg Empire and other states was inefficient. Russia avoided revolution in 1848 and was arguably the most repressive of the European states. It might equally be true that other European governments did not use the instruments of law and order as effectively as they could have done: the Prussian army could have been used more effectively in Berlin in 1848, and the National Guard could have controlled Paris more firmly.

It is necessary to explain some of the new political ideas of which the European ruling classes were so wary. These new political ideas, which had developed from the middle of the eighteenth century, can be categorised under four headings: liberalism, democracy, socialism and nationalism.

Liberalism in the nineteenth century was the belief that government should be carried on by means involving consent among the various sections of society or the nation. Liberalism's intellectual justification was derived from eighteenth-century rationalism, which had attacked all forms of arbitrary power, particularly the power of kings. Liberals believed that the power of traditional institutions, such as the Church and the monarchy, should be restrained by institutions representing the interests of society more generally and the aristocracy and the more wealthy sections of the middle class in particular. The liberal programme – government by parliament or representative assembly, freedom of the press and individual freedom – was most popular among the emerging classes of manufacturers, merchants and professionals, who saw the privileges of the Church and the most wealthy sections of the aristocracy as obstacles to their own economic and social betterment [**doc. 2a**]. Liberals, as distinct from those who preached democracy, believed in the sovereignty of parliament rather than the sovereignty of the people. Middle-class liberals regarded democracy with suspicion, since it was associated in their minds with the excesses of the First French Republic. Consequently middle-class liberals in both Britain and France advocated broadening the property franchise: '*Vox populi, vox dei*, which gives to the majority the infallibility of God . . . is the most dangerous and most despotic absurdity that has ever emerged from the human brain. If you want to ruin a state give it universal suffrage', so claimed Odilon Barot, leader of the Dynastic Opposition in the 1840s.

It was the campaign of Barot and Adolphe Thiers in the Chamber of Deputies, initially against the government of Guizot, that eventually led to a major campaign for parliamentary reform. Barot and Thiers were unsuccessful, and subsequently the campaign for extending the franchise was taken up by Laurent-Antoine Paguerre, a publisher, at the end of May 1847. He was the dominant figure of the Comité Central des Electeurs de la Seine, a committee originally set up in the 1846 election to organise opposition candidates. It was from this originally modest movement that the campaign of the Banqueteers developed. The first political banquet was held on 9 July 1847, and it was addressed by Paguerre and Barot (**65**). (Thiers would not associate himself with the banquets as he regarded them as politically inflammatory. He was, in fact, proved correct as the banquets were taken over by those demanding republican and democratic reforms.) Originally the banquets were a classic example of middle-class liberal reform, and the Banqueteers owed much to the Anti-Corn Law League in Britain.

Elsewhere on the European mainland, with the important exception of Belgium, liberalism had made little headway either in the form of government concessions or in men's minds. This is hardly surprising if the lack of development of a middle class east of the Rhine is taken into account. But, of course, wherever urban middle-class life did develop, there grew up alongside it a liberal ideology. For example, in Italy, ideas of economic liberalism were put forward by Romagnosi, in Lombardy, where there was some commercial progress. In addition it was the concessions to liberal reform by Pius IX in the Papal States that produced an atmosphere of excitement and demands for reform that forced the monarchs of Italy to grant constitutions and generally to liberalise their régimes. Thus part of the immediate background to the revolutions of 1848 in France and Italy was a demand for moderate reform. It is now necessary to examine some of the more far-reaching programmes and show how they became more significant in an environment of economic disaster.

Democracy in the early nineteenth century was the belief in universal male suffrage as a method of expressing the general will of the people. Thus, theoretically at least, there was no need for traditional institutions such as monarchy; ultimately therefore democrats were republicans, as they believed in the abolition of monarchy. It was these ideas that motivated the Jacobins in France and had led to the execution of Louis XVI in 1793. Democracy continued to appeal to the urban working class in the early nineteenth century, and some republicans made a conscious appeal to the working class: 'To the workers! To their indefensible rights, to their sacred interests, up to the present unrecognised', declared Ledru-Rollin at a banquet in Lille in 1847. However, the attitude of the bourgeois republican politicians towards the power of the working class was often ambivalent. The possibility of a repetition of the excesses of the Revolutionary Terror of 1792 was something that lingered on in the minds of the respectable classes. Thus, although Ledru-Rollin was seen as the reincarnation of the Terror by the *noblesse* and the *grande bourgeoisie*, as Minister of the Interior in 1848 he was not so enthusiastic about working-class rights as he had been in 1847. When the people of Paris entered the Chamber of Deputies in May 1848, Ledru-Rollin no doubt saw the spectre of mob rule, and it was this that encouraged him to call for order; de Tocqueville, in describing the scene, said that Ledru-Rollin was 'hooted down' and forced to leave the 'rostrum' (**7**). Apparently, then, even radical republicans like Ledru-Rollin believed that parliament came before the will of the people and that political reform must precede social amelioration.

Those who argued that some kind of social reform or change was necessary over and above political reform were, in the 1830s and 1840s, called socialists. Socialism was not at this time a clearly defined doctrine. Indeed, its development as a clearly articulated ideology was only in its infancy. The term 'socialist' had been used first by Robert Owen, the English philanthropist, in the *Co-operative Magazine* of 1827 (**27**). His thinking about economics owed much to Adam Smith, but was, at the same time, infused with moral notions of the just deserts of labour. Owen claimed that the value of any commodity was determined by both the present and the past labour that had gone into it. (Past labour had produced existing capital or stock.) These ideas were to be explained and extended in more scientific terms by Ricardo and, more significantly for subsequent history, by Karl Marx. If the value of a commodity was determined by the amount of present and past labour that was involved, then the great moral problem, Owen claimed, was whether the capital, the accumulation of past labour, should be individually owned or commonly owned and controlled. Thus, there was the basis of socialism: the common ownership of the means of production, distribution and exchange.

The great problem that faced those who believed that common ownership was socially just was how to achieve their ends. Thus many people, particularly in England, who were called socialist in the 1840s may have advocated social reform, philanthropy or cooperation only according to the thinking of Owen. In France, however, the common ownership of the 'fruits of the earth' was for some men only to be achieved by violent insurrection. Here was a fusion of a revolutionary tradition with ideas of social as well as political equality. Foremost in the conspiratorial revolutionary tradition in France in the 1830s and 1840s were the secret societies, inspired by Auguste Blanqui. It was to this revolutionary tradition that Marx and Engels were referring in their Communist Manifesto produced in the year of the revolutions, 1848. Writing much later Engels observed that, believing in violent revolution as the only solution to the condition of the working class, it would have been impossible to write a 'Socialist Manifesto', since socialism was the theory of the respectable middle-class doctrinaires. The word 'communism' however, was far from respectable, as it carried the connotations of insurrection and militancy [**doc. 2f**].

Between those whom Marx and Engels would have regarded as middle-class doctrinaires and social reformers, like Owen in England and Charles Fourier in France, and the advocates of proletarian revolution, like themselves, were those who saw the power of the state as capable of dispensing social justice. Louis Blanc was probably the most important advocate of this philosophy, and he was to play an important part in the Provisional Government that was established after the abdication of Louis Philippe in France. Blanc believed that the state should regulate the economy, an idea derived from Saint-Simon, and that the state should guarantee the 'right to work'. Thus Blanc was adopting what later became a social democratic position – that socialist reforms could be achieved democratically through the election of socialist representatives – which was quite distinct from the social revolutionary or communist stance adopted by Blanqui and Marx.

Clearly the various ideas enveloped under the heading 'socialism' were, in the 1830s and 1840s, not always consistent with one another. Consequently 'socialism' as an ideological force that motivated men in the revolutions of 1848 should not be overestimated. It was probably more significant in France than anywhere else. Liberalism and democracy, and particularly the former in the minds of the rising middle class, were much more potent political ideas immediately before 1848, simply because liberalism had had some measure of success in France, Britain and Belgium from 1830 onwards. Equally powerful, especially east of the Rhine, was nationalism. Nationalism, the fourth of the major political forces transforming European society, was essentially a liberal political philosophy.

Nationalists believed that a group of people, because of a common language, a common history, heritage, culture and possibly religion, should be brought together to form a nation state [**docs 2b,c**]. Britain and France were already nation states in this sense. After 1815 those who hoped to form a national Italy or a national Germany were for the most part liberal, since the constitution of a national state involved consent within society about a form of government. Nationalism had at first been given a great impetus by Jacobin ideas of democracy. Obviously 'sovereignty of the people' could be construed as a nationalist idea as well as a democratic one, as presumably 'a people' would have to unite together in order to achieve sovereignty. Further, the Napoleonic conquests provoked a sense of nationalism in those parts of Europe that came within the French empire, especially the Confederation of the Rhine and the Italian states. However, the excesses of the Revolutionary Terror may have discredited democracy; consequently after 1815 nationalism was probably more liberal than democratic.

In the late eighteenth century the stirrings of nationalism were apparent in central and southern Europe. In Germany Johann Herder had advanced the notion of *volkgeist* or 'national soul', by which he meant a consciousness that produced a particular language, art, culture, particular forms of thinking, customs and traditions. Not surprisingly, therefore, the early stirrings of nationalism manifested themselves in the activities of the middle classes and the gentry and more specifically the educated élite [**doc. 2c**]. Historical writing was a means of establishing national identity: the Czech Frantisek Palacký was writing a history of Bohemia before the revolutions of 1848, and in 1842 Szafarzik published his *Slavonic Ethnography*. In Italy the historical novels of Alessandro Manzoni recalled the past greatness of Italy, but obviously appealed only to the literate minority.

In political terms this cultural renaissance, or *Risorgimento*, which formed the intellectual springs of nationalism, was directed against the power of the Habsburgs. The 1815 settlement had made the Habsburg Empire the most powerful political unit in Europe. The territorial extent of the Empire meant that Metternich's principal political task was the handling of the many subject peoples. Thus the Italians of Lombardy and Venetia, which were part of the Habsburg Empire, saw Italian nationalism primarily in terms of establishing their independence from the Habsburgs. This was also true of the Magyars, who, under the leadership of Kossuth, were to make one of the most concerted attempts to establish their independence from Habsburg rule in 1848–49.

However, just as socialism was a term that covered a considerable diversity of political formulae, so too was nationalism. This diversity of ideas was most apparent in Italy, where Mazzini's republican and revolutionary nationalism vied with Gioberti's idea of a federation of Italian states under the leadership of the Pope. There were also the ideas of economic cooperation between Italian states put forward by Romagnosi, which no doubt owed much to the example of the Zollverein of German states. Ultimately the most realistic form of Italian nationalism that appeared before 1848 was that put forward by D'Azeglio, a leading politician in Piedmont. D'Azeglio advocated a federation of Italian states under Piedmontese leadership. In the long run the primacy of the state of Piedmont determined the method whereby Italian unification was achieved.

The important thing to remember about nationalism in the period before 1848 was that it was still very much at an embryonic stage. Nationalists were unable to coordinate their diverse programmes. The protracted discussions of the men at the Frankfurt National Assembly in 1848 are proof of this point. Thus, like socialism and democracy, and to a lesser extent like liberalism, nationalism was a political force still in its early stages of development. Nonetheless all these ideas – liberalism, democracy, socialism and nationalism – were new forces gnawing away at the stability of European society. The ruling classes regarded them all as dangerous but very often proved incapable of effectively suppressing them, particularly when the economic condition of Europe began to deteriorate in the 1840s. It is here that the great paradox of the 1848 revolutions is to be discovered, for although the discussions about the various forms of government came to the fore in the assemblies that emerged in that year, the revolutions were in fact made by those classes who were for the most part untouched by the general range of liberal ideologies. It was the working class who died on the barricades:

> In Berlin there were only about fifteen [middle-class] represen-
> tatives, about thirty master craftsmen among the three hundred
> victims of the March fighting; in Milan, only twelve students,
> white collar workers or landlords among the 350 dead of the insur-
> rection. It was their hunger [i.e. of the poor] which powered the
> demonstrations that turned into revolution (**20**).

What was it then, that happened in the 1840s, which brought about a
state of affairs likely to cause vast numbers of the poor sections of the
population to take to the streets?

6 The Crisis of the 1840s

There is no doubt that the general economic condition of Europe deteriorated in the 1840s, particularly after 1845–46. The precise nature of this deterioration, and therefore its effect on different classes of the population, has been hotly disputed by historians. Simply put, it can be said that the widespread agricultural crisis caused by crop failures brought rapid increases in the price of grain and bread [doc. 4]. These price increases were further compounded by the effects of a potato blight. This food crisis drastically affected the standard of living of the working class and the peasantry. There was also a financial and commercial crisis, especially in France, depressing primarily the confidence and livelihood of the investing class, and ultimately causing an increase in unemployment in the industrial towns of Lille, Roubaix, Tourcoing and Mulhouse, where many of the mills were forced to close down (60).

It makes sense to look at the agricultural crisis first, since changes in food prices affected the poor, the majority of the population, most profoundly. Remembering that approximately 70 per cent of working-class income was spent on food at this time, rises in the price of grain by 100 to 150 per cent in the space of a year had a devastating effect on the condition of a class whose existence was already precarious. Price rises were probably most marked in France, but there were dramatic increases elsewhere. For instance, the price of grain in Hamburg rose by almost 60 per cent between 1845 and 1847, as did the cost of rye [doc. 4]. The poor condition of workers in Germany was also attested to by contemporaries, as in the case of J. J. Dittrich who claimed in 1847: 'Not a small number of the inhabitants of the province which is called the pearl of the crown of Prussia, Silesia, live far worse than the convicts in the prisons' (25), [docs 3a–e]. It is important, too, to look at the price of other starch food which formed the substantial part of the diet of the poor, particularly potatoes. The price of potatoes in some German towns increased by as much as 135 per cent between 1846 and 1847, and there is no doubt that the lower classes in the towns and in the countryside became increasingly impoverished and demoralised [docs 2a–e].

This food crisis manifested itself before 1848 with food riots in Leyden, the Hague, Delft and Harlem in 1845 (**43**). The effects of the potato blight were also felt in Belgium, causing a considerable migration of workers into north-eastern France, which only served to exacerbate the existing unemployment there.

The grain crisis in France was considerable, causing a large increase in the amount of imported grain between 1846 and 1847. In 1846 the French imported grain to the value of 125 million francs, and by 1847 this had increased to 231 million francs. Grain was imported chiefly through the ports of Marseille and Arles; but the rail link from Paris to Lyons and Marseille was incomplete. This explains the patchiness of the economic map of France and there were vast differences in the price of grain between the northern and central districts. In fact it has been pointed out that the coastal regions were not dramatically affected by food shortages (**47**). Nonetheless, the effects of the food crisis were extremely severe, debilitating a vast section of the European population that was ill-equipped to face such a difficult crisis [**doc. 4**].

As has already been indicated, the European peasantry had been subjected to the shortages of land and food over a considerable period. The food crisis of 1846 and 1847 was not just a short-term disaster that happened to spark off a few demonstrations that by chance turned into revolutions. The general inadequacy of the land as far as food production was concerned had caused migration on a vast scale, not only from the German states, as has already been mentioned, but from all parts of Europe. The effects of this migration on the existing urban populations were disturbing. The impact on Paris is extremely important. Not only did Paris undergo a vast population increase in the first half of the nineteenth century, but a substantial proportion of this increase was due to immigration. The population of Paris increased from 713,966 in 1817 to 1,053,897 in 1846. More startling is the fact that the increase of population between 1841 and 1846 was in the region of 12.56 per cent, with immigration into the city much higher in the period 1841–46 than in the period 1836–41. The majority of this immigrant population was itinerant, as shown by the vast increase in the numbers living in lodging-houses in the central districts. In 1831 the lodging-house population was 23,150, and by 1846 it had increased to 50,007 (**52**). By far the largest section of this itinerant population was male, and therefore constituted a vast pool of potentially violent rioters. Working-class life was noted for its brutality at this time, and there was much conflict between the new arrivals and the established population. Thus it is unrealistic to see the explosion of the working class in 1848 merely as the result of a food crisis producing a revolution. There was already a long tradition of violence in an urban environment that had been deteriorating throughout the period 1830–46, due to a vast increase in population and a decline in the available stock of housing. This set of circumstances may actually explain how and by what means a population took to the streets and overthrew the existing provisions of law and order (*32, 52*).

Conditions in France were made worse by the financial crisis. Trade depressions had already been experienced in 1827–32 and 1837–42. It was in the sector of railway building that the problems of the French economy had become evident. In 1841 Guizot's government had passed a statute facilitating compulsory purchase of land for the purpose of railway building. Consequently investors had been encouraged to put their savings into railway building and metallurgical industries generally. This caused a vast increase in iron output, which resulted in overproduction and consequently considerable surpluses. In 1847 iron production fell by about 30 per cent. Coal production fell by 20 per cent over the same period. The final crisis in confidence was reflected by dramatic falls in share prices on the Bourse. Since the government had invested over 600 million francs in railways, local road building and the rebuilding of the fortifications of Paris, it also became a crisis of confidence in the government. The press were quick to seize upon this: 'It is the government which has precipitated this condition of ruin' (*47*). The financial crisis thus synchronised with the political discontent already apparent in the Banqueteers' campaign for electoral reform.

The reformers also found another stick with which to beat the government when two cases of corruption became apparent. First, in 1847 there was the criminal trial of a former Minister of Public Works, Teste, who had used his office to procure industrial concessions. Second, there was the case of the duc de Praslin, who battered his wife to death for the love of an English governess. He was brought to trial but succeeded in committing suicide. These two cases of corruption had the effect of invigorating the opposition to Guizot's government and 'together these cases were taken as a revelation of the manner of life of the governing classes' (*53, 72*). Confidence in Guizot's government rapidly eroded, so that the comfortable majority of 248 votes to 84 votes on the speech from the throne in 1846 was reduced to 43 by February 1848. Clearly the food crisis, coming at the end of a long period of disruption and demoralisation for the poor, had the effect of mobilising discontent against the government, not just Guizot's government but probably any government. This discontent was fairly indiscriminate. The financial crisis on the other hand had a much more specific effect, as it alienated the middle-class support that Louis Philippe and his ministers would normally have relied on in a crisis. As Labrousse has put it so succinctly: 'Several instabilities coincided' (**47**). Nor was the financial crisis exclusively confined to France. In Germany a depression in the textile industry resulted in a 40 per cent fall in the export of unbleached yarn from the Zollverein states between 1844 and 1847 (**79**).

The severity of these trade depressions served to stimulate the growing appetite for liberalism among the middle class, especially among the lower middle class or *petite bourgeoisie* in France. The great power of the working class, more apparent than real, as time proved, persuaded the established ruling classes to surrender power with little fight in the early months of 1848. The ensuing months displayed the attempts of these two hitherto politically and socially underprivileged classes – the workers and the lower middle class – to compete for power. Although certain causes were more relevant in some places than others – the financial crisis was more pertinent to France than to the Habsburg lands, for instance – the widespread nature of the revolutions suggests certain common explanations. The great common denominator was the town. The cities provided the stage – for the cities had vast concentrations of poor people, far more likely to act together than their rural counterparts, and were also the centres of political power. Significantly, the Provisional Government in France was proclaimed at the Hotel de Ville in Paris and not at one of the royal palaces. It was ultimately on the cities that the great social and economic developments – population growth, industrialisation, railway building – rebounded. It was to the cities that the political exiles made their way. Mazzini had founded the League of Exiles in Paris in 1834. It was in the cities that the liberal and national aspirations were voiced. The inability of the ruling classes to control these cities effectively in a period of rapid social and economic change provides the key to the revolutions of 1848.

Part Three: 1848 The Year of Revolution

A striking feature of the 1848 revolutions was the rapidity of success they enjoyed, only to be followed by speedy defeat. In Paris, Louis Philippe had abdicated on 24 February, and two days later the socialist, Louis Blanc, announced the establishment of the National Workshops which would provide work for the unemployed at the rate of two francs a day. On 3 March the Hungarian nationalist, Kossuth, made his famous speech at Pressburg demanding parliamentary government and a decentralisation of the Habsburg Imperial Administration. Within a fortnight, Metternich, the personification of order and stability, who had dominated Austrian and European politics for so long, had resigned as Austrian Chancellor and was secretly making his way to England. In Prussia the capitulation of Frederick William IV to the revolution was no less rapid. Within months, however, these early successes, greeted with heady enthusiasm, had been forgotten and had given way to conflict, recriminations, mistrust and eventually defeat for the original revolutionary principles. In June 1848 the National Guard acted barbarously against the people of Paris and the National Workshops were abolished. Louis Blanc was powerless. To all intents and purposes the French Second Republic was at an end, although it would appear to have taken a long time dying. In Austria the Habsburgs found a saviour in Schwarzenberg, who became Chancellor in the autumn of 1848, determined to crush the revolutions and re-establish monarchical authority. The deliberations of the German liberals at Frankfurt continued into 1849 but they had no real power to implement their decisions.

In order to understand the essential feature of the 1848 revolutions it is necessary to carry out a state by state examination. Nevertheless one general observation can be made at the outset which may serve to underpin the more detailed explanations that follow: the initial demands of the different classes in society stemmed from separate and distinct social and economic grievances. Thus as the revolutions progressed and these grievances were not ameliorated or were redressed, as the case may be, then the original cohesion of the revolutionaries, which was often tenuous anyway, was finally dissipated. This applied in France between the classes and in central and southern Europe between the races.

7 France

De Tocqueville in his famous *Recollections* wrote how, on 24 February 1848, he returned home after Louis Philippe's abdication to find his brother and his sister-in-law waiting in his house. He recalled that his sister-in-law had lost her head. 'She already saw her husband dead and her daughters raped' (7). De Tocqueville promptly arranged for his sister-in-law to leave Paris for the safety of the countryside. Such happenings were probably not uncommon among the *grands bourgeois* families of Paris, and Marx and Engels had certainly hit the right note in their Communist Manifesto, first published in February 1848, when they crowed: 'Let the ruling classes tremble at a Communistic revolution' (3). But the fear and anticipation of the respectable classes was probably greater than events warranted. The February Revolution was a relatively bloodless affair, with only those who took to the streets risking death. The new Provisional Government was made up of moderate men, and even the socialist Louis Blanc would be condemned by later generations of more revolutionary socialists as having been unprepared and probably too soft. Nevertheless bourgeois fear of what the revolution represented was decisive in determining the subsequent history of the French Second Republic. In particular it explains the steady movement to the right that resulted eventually in the election of Louis Napoleon as the Republic's first and only President.

The policies pursued by the new Provisional Government were essentially moderate. The leading member of the government, Lamartine, was no Robespierre, and he sought moderate solutions. He was by nature a cautious man and he had no grand designs or great schemes like Blanc. Nor did he possess the grasp of political and administrative detail that was the gift of Ledru-Rollin, the Minister of the Interior. Lamartine became Minister of Foreign Affairs and the conduct of foreign relations, or rather the principles on which foreign relations should be conducted, was a matter that consumed much of the Provisional Government's time. This may seem surprising since it had been the acute social and economic disorders that had brought people on to the streets of Paris. As far as Lamartine was concerned, however, the unemployed would have to trust in Louis Blanc. In the meantime, the first priority was to show that the France of 1848 was not the France of 1792. French Republican armies were not going to make war on the rest of Europe. Understandably Lamartine's Manifesto to Europe, issued within two weeks of Louis Philippe's abdication, was a document intended to allay the fears of the other powers. 'Half a century', Lamartine wrote, 'separates 1792 from 1848. To return after the lapse of half a century to the principle of 1792, or to the principle of conquest pursued during the Empire, would not be to advance, but to retrogress. . . . The world and ourselves are desirous of advancing to fraternity and peace. . .'(2). Such was Lamartine's caution. It is also an indication of the extent to which French politicians deferred to the past.

Once the threat of foreign intervention had been removed it was possible for the Provisional Government to attend to the other important questions. Apart from diplomacy there were the three main issues of finance, political consolidation of the régime, and the social question. In all three areas the government was found lacking, although, to be fair, the difficulty of consolidating the republican régime in the face of the political and social conservatism of rural France was extreme. Further, the solutions sought by the government often only created more of the same type of problems or exacerbated existing ones. This was certainly the case in financial matters. It had been a financial disaster that had caused Louis Philippe's government to forfeit bourgeois support: the Provisional Government was not sufficiently successful in capturing bourgeois confidence in the weeks and months immediately after February. Uncertainty continued to prevail in the business world and this was reflected by a dramatic decline in the normally stable share index of the Bank of France. There had also been a considerable decline in gold reserves – from 226 million francs in February to 59 million francs by mid-March (59). The combined effect of the fall of the Bank of France's share index and the shrinkage of gold reserves was to restrict lending facilities to commercial and provincial banks, resulting in a general strangulation of credit facilities. This was to have serious social consequences. Immediately, however, a decline in the fortunes of the country's national bank meant automatically a decline in the financial stability of the government itself. In fact the government's deficit rose rapidly during March and consequently a 45 centime tax on direct income was introduced. The tax fell predominantly on the landed classes and its effects were most severely felt by the smaller farmers and peasant proprietors. In the subsequent elections for the Constituent Assembly rural France squarely rejected republicanism. Whether this was due exclusively to the 45 centime tax or to clerical influence does not matter. The effect was to make the consolidation of the republican régime more difficult. The failure of the Provisional Government to introduce a single agricultural reform was a glaring fault, and the problems of collecting the 45 centime tax were extreme. In the Department of Lot, for instance, it was necessary for the authorities to call in the army on no less than nine occasions in order to secure the collection of the hated tax (**17**).

On the question of political consolidation the Provisional Government was no more successful. As Minister of the Interior, Ledru-Rollin was responsible for the organisation of the elections for the Constituent Assembly which, the republicans hoped, would draw up a comprehensive republican constitution and so validate the revolution of February. On 2 March the Provisional Government introduced universal suffrage, thus enfranchising nine million new voters. The idealism of democracy told the republicans that the panacea of universal suffrage would deliver France into a new age. The more cynical observed that France had now been delivered into the hands of a fickle peasantry. More correctly, it might be said that the fate of France now rested with the Church, for although the clergy welcomed the demise of Louis Philippe they were less than pleased with ensuing demands from socialists and radical republicans for an end to Church control of primary education (**67**). It was hardly surprising then that clerical opposition to republicanism in the Constituent Assembly elections of April was nothing less than implacable. The bishops drew up lists of acceptable candidates which in turn the priests recommended to their parishioners [**doc. 7**]. For their part, the republicans, particularly those to the left, had argued for a delay in the holding of the elections in order to provide the opportunity of educating the electorate along republican lines. Further, Ledru-Rollin had done his best to carry out an administrative purge by dismissing monarchist prefects and replacing them with republicans (**66**). It would be fair to say, then, that the elections were a struggle between republican bureaucracy and clerical influence. Ultimately clericalism was a far more durable and entrenched tradition than republicanism (**53**).

Unfortunately for the republicans the elections were held on Easter Sunday, when the presence of clerics within village communities would have been distinctly obvious. Leaving aside the weight of clerical pressure, it is hardly surprising that a politically inexperienced electorate should have expressed a preference for familiar local notables. This would certainly have been the case in one department, where ninety-seven candidates contested seven seats. (**70**). There was also intense provincial hostility to anything that emanated from Paris, and that included republicanism. Thus the result of the elections, although disappointing to the republicans, was not altogether surprising. Over half the deputies elected were on the right: 200 Orleanists, 150 legitimists and a further 350 committed to the clerical campaign for freedom of education. Of the remainder, about 250 were for the most part moderate republicans and there were some 70 to 80 radical and socialist republicans. But perhaps a more telling point was that some 700 of the 900 deputies paid tax in excess of 500 francs per annum (**53**). The political centre of gravity of the Constituent Assembly, then, was certainly weighted towards the interests of property, and any willingness on the part of a deputy to accept the label 'moderate republican' may not have been particularly revealing in terms of his political attitude or intention.

An assembly so comprehensively dominated by men of property was unlikely to be radical in dealing with the other great priority facing the Second Republic: the social problem. Moreover the conservative elements of society were beginning to recover from the initial shock of the February upheaval, and a conservative majority in the Assembly no doubt increased bourgeois confidence. The essence of the social problem was unemployment, which was probably still quite high by the spring of 1848. Any hopes of wide-ranging public works were dashed when the Constituent Assembly insisted that the Provisional Government be replaced by a new five-man Executive Commission of which Louis Blanc was not a member. There was also considerable opposition to the National Workshops and the leading spokesman of the right on this question, the Comte de Falloux, saw in the Workshops the potential for future revolutionary outbreaks. Consequently the demand by the radicals and socialists for programmes of public works to alleviate unemployment went unheeded. Further, moderate republicans like Lamartine also feared the radical demand for a war to liberate Poland. On 15 May a crowd of workers led by politicians from the radical clubs gathered outside the Assembly building. Eventually the crowd surged into the main body of the hall and broke up the meeting, and one of the club leaders, Aloysius Huber, proclaimed a new Provisional Government. If this was a planned uprising, with the radicals hoping that Parisian workers would follow their lead, then it was a vain hope. Nevertheless it did give the government the excuse to arrest a number of radical leaders and it was now becoming clear that the radicals were becoming more and more isolated. The counter-revolution had already begun, for in the previous month fifty-nine workers had been killed by troops in Rouen after a protest about the failure of the radicals in the elections (**59**).

Contemporary opinion saw society becoming increasingly divided by April–May 1848 and it was in these circumstances that on 28 May [**docs 8a–c**], the Club de la Montagne de Montmartre called for a people's banquet in direct imitation of the bourgeois banquets which had been held in 1847. The Assembly detected in such an event a likelihood of disorder and its organisers were promptly arrested (**63**). In the following month the Assembly announced its intention to ditch the scheme of National Workshops. The rumours of a workers' insurrection which had permeated the police reports for the previous weeks [**docs 8b, c**] were now confirmed. The workers set up barricades [**doc. 9a**]. Cavaignac's troops, acting for the government, were ruthless in their suppression of the uprising. Initially the revolutionaries lost some 400 to 500 men, but those who fled were flushed out from the narrow alleyways of Paris and some 3,000 were cut down. The Russian exile Alexander Herzen, who witnessed the event, observed that Russian Cossack troops were as meek as lambs compared with the barbarous French soldiers (**12**). A further 11,693 people were charged, and many of them were deported to Algeria (**32**).

The 'June Days' uprising was a remarkable incident in the history of the Second Republic because it revealed the divisons of French society in an emphatic way. Marx and de Tocqueville are agreed on this [**docs 9b,c**]. The conclusions of contemporary observers are not always accepted at their face value by modern historians and the interpretation of the June Days demonstrates this point well. An examination of the occupations of those who were arrested has not produced conclusions that can be asserted with the certainty held by Marx and de Tocqueville. Rudé's examination of those arrested revealed that there was a significant similarity to those trades which had been involved in the storming of the Bastille in 1789. There were 554 stonemasons, 510 joiners, 283 painters, 140 carpenters along with large numbers of cabinet makers, locksmiths and jewellers. Rudé further contends that independent craftsmen outnumbered wage-earners, or new Proletarians in the Marxist sense, by about two to one. From this he concludes that the June Days conflict was not strictly a modern class conflict, a polarisation between bourgeoisie and proletariat. Rather it was a more traditional form of protest by older independent crafts and small producers. Nevertheless he does accept that transport workers and *mécaniciens* (engineering workers), part of the newer wage-earning proletariat, provided the militant hard core for the insurgents, although he doubts that the Parisian proletariat was fully formed (32). More recent examinations of the participants in the June Days uprising have produced conclusions that are more closely aligned with those of Marx (60). It has been found that certain groups figure more prominently within the numbers that were arrested than their representation within the population as a whole would warrant. Consequently although it is agreed that building workers (stonemasons, carpenters and joiners) were conspicuous in their participation it is emphasised that other groups were disproportionately prominent – metal workers, leather workers, transport workers and, to a lesser extent, printing workers and those involved in chemicals. It is also stressed that the insurgents came disproportionately from those workers employed in the larger firms and workshops, although it would appear that Parisian industry still tended to be on a small scale. Further, the building, metals and leather trades had quite a well established tradition of organisation and cooperation. It would seem then that Marx's contention has a degree of statistical substantiation that until recently historians have not recognised.

There are other considerations to take into account. What, for instance, was the rôle of migrant workers in the events of June? Most of those arrested were immigrants from other parts of France (52, 59, 60). For the most part these immigrants came from north-eastern France (59, 60) where they may have already experienced the industrial way of life. Rural Frenchmen, except those from departments immediately contiguous to Paris, were apparently less likely to move to Paris. However, there were a number of those arrested who had been born in eastern France and the Massif Central. Those who supported the army and the Garde Mobile were very often peasant volunteers, who had come in from outside Paris, together with shopkeepers, merchants and landlords (60). It should not be thought that peasant outsiders were always on the side of reaction, although this may have been generally so in the case of those who came to Paris. Elsewhere, for instance in Marseille, the more recently arrived often supplied the groups of politically active democrats, republicans and socialists. The artisans of Marseille had traditionally been clerical and royalist in their allegiance. This ceased to be so from the 1840s and this political shift has largely been attributed to *étrangers* (or immigrants) many of whom were of peasant stock (75). The case of Marseille reveals strikingly the effects of demography and migration on the political behaviour of the poorer sections of the population, for in

Marseille there was considerable hostility towards Italian immigrant labour. In the north-east – in Lille and Roubaix especially – there was resentment of Belgian workers (**69, 76**) while worker riots in Alsace were often anti-semitic in character.

The traditionalism of rural communities was probably much stronger than in the growing urban centres, and the activities of the peasantry during the Second Republic would seem to confirm this. They were primarily concerned with defending their ancient rights, as in the Pyrenees where there were numerous peasant riots protesting against the Forest Codes of 1827 and 1837 which had denied them traditional privileges of hunting and foraging. There were similar outbreaks in the Alpine Region and the Massif Central (**59**).

There is a sense in which concentration on the June Days in order to discover the basic divisions of French society can be misleading. Most Frenchmen lived in small market towns economically closely connected to the land. Even larger centres like Paris were still subject to sharp fluctuations in the prices of agricultural produce. This was because most towns, Paris included, were economically dependent on their immediate hinterlands, since railway and road communications were still limited. The Paris Basin and northern France were essentially grain-growing areas and it was a crisis in grain that was the central feature of 1847 and 1848 (**47, 69**). In that sense, then, the social crisis in Paris was probably a pre-industrial crisis rather than the kind of crisis suggested by Marx. Nevertheless, the concentration of political power in Paris makes it natural that events in the capital should be seen as important. The fact remains that the politicians of the Assembly saw in the Workshops a source of insurrection, and their decision to dissolve the Workshops was conclusive.

The political consequences of the June Days are much easier to chart. There was a further inexorable shift to the right revealed first by the trust placed by the Assembly in Cavaignac and secondly by the growing popularity of Louis Napoleon. The myth of Bonapartism was powerful among the peasantry, and politicians like Molé and Thiers believed that Louis Napoleon could be controlled and that his popularity could be used to defend the fabric of society. The name of Bonaparte was intimately connected with order, which was the quest for most Frenchmen after June. Bonapartism's appeal cut right across all social classes of society with the exception of the more modest businessmen and some of the more radical working class. Protestant businessmen in the north and east of France are reckoned to have been markedly anti-Bonapartist (**59**). What then was the appeal of Louis Napoleon? Primarily there was of course the legend of the great Bonaparte that was so much a part of popular culture. It was a name associated with national glory which was very attractive in the aftermath of a régime which had been remarkably unsuccessful in foreign affairs. Many of the older peasants would have remembered the Empire as a period of prosperity as well as glory, and may have compared it wistfully with their current misfortunes – depression in agriculture and the 45 centime tax. Thus peasant support for Louis Napoleon was as much a protest against Republican taxation policy as against anything else. In the summer and autumn of 1848 Louis Napoleon spoke openly of his support for religious education and the Papacy and consequently hired some very powerful election agents for the forthcoming presidential elections which were to be held in December. But for the most part the vote for Louis Napoleon stemmed from negative calculations: a vote for Louis Napoleon by the working class was a vote against Cavaignac, the 'butcher of June'; many legitimist notables were attracted to Bonapartism simply because businessmen and entrepreneurs were committed to Cavaignac (**61**). Finally the presidential elections of December revealed a vote for order. Louis Napoleon polled well over five million votes and Cavaignac well over a million. Their nearest rival was Ledru-Rollin with a mere 370,119 votes. Both Cavaignac and Louis Napoleon were men of order. The former had proved his commitment to order by action, while the latter aspired to such a commitment through the power of a legend.

Once Louis Napoleon had been elected President, the Constituent Assembly voted for its own dissolution in January 1849. Louis Napoleon's first Cabinet was dominated by legitimists and Orleanists led by Odilon Barrot, leader of the Dynastic Opposition immediately before February 1848. Louis Napoleon was now in a position to consolidate his hold over French government and society. He resorted to traditional methods of administrative manipulation and purged the prefecture of its republican personnel. Despite such precautions the elections for the new Legislative Assembly held in May 1849 still produced a surprising republican representation. There were some 75– 80 moderate republicans and a further 180 radical and socialist republicans. Conservative deputies were still in a majority, winning about 500 seats, 200 being won by legitimists. The conservative representation was comprised socially of notables and wealthy magnates. They viewed the continued presence of left-wing republicans – *montagnards* – with alarm. The republican caucus was based in the towns, in parts of the Massif Central, in the valleys of the Saône and Rhône, in the Midi, in Aquitaine and the Pyrenees. The apparent danger of the left may have been magnified by its geographical concentration. Although the numerical representation of the left-wing republicans was considerable, their ability to take determined political action was insignificant. They did in fact attempt an insurrection on 13 June 1849 in protest at French republican troops being sent to Rome to restore the Papacy. The insurrection was an abortive failure, its only effect being to reinforce the resolve of the conservatives to carry out a policy of repression. By the following year the conservatives were in the ascendancy when in May the Legislative Assembly disenfranchised all those who had court records, and all those who did not fulfil a three-year residential qualification. It was an action directed against what Thiers regarded as the 'vile multitude', and of course it greatly reduced the active voting support of the left-wing republicans (59).

If Molé and Thiers believed that they could continue their manipulation of Napoleon at will they were soon to be disillusioned. The movement towards dictatorship was quickening. Bonapartism had gained considerable support within the Assembly and Louis Napoleon kept up a vigorous propaganda by a series of provincial tours. Eventually, in December 1851, a carefully planned coup effectively overthrew the Republic. There was resistance – workers in Paris put up barricades – but it was easily crushed. In the provinces there were pockets of resistance, though much of the peasant activity is difficult to interpret. The actions of the peasantry and small town-dwellers was certainly desperate. They attacked the houses of money-lenders and tax collectors, destroying papers and account books. In the village of Taigny the people attacked the church and smashed the confessionals, claiming that they had been used by the priests as places in which to secretly fornicate with women of the village (59). Such was the elemental nature of peasant discontent. It stemmed from frustration with economic privation and uncertainty. It was also uncoordinated, and the odds against the urban revolutionary republicans were militarily too great. The Second Republic had come to an end.

8 The Habsburg Lands

If there are such things as turning points in history then nine o'clock in the evening on 13 March 1848 must surely qualify for that status in the history of the Habsburg Empire. It was then that Metternich, the Austrian Chancellor, tendered his resignation to the Emperor Ferdinand. Metternich was the symbol of the old order and his name was synonymous with the Settlement of 1815. His fall was the result of a coincidence of two different historical trends. On the one hand his resignation was a response to the clamour for liberal reform which had reached a crescendo with the news of the revolution in Paris. The Habsburg Court needed to sacrifice someone if it was to have any credence with the nationalities, particularly the Magyars. On the other hand Metternich's resignation was also a response to a conspiracy from within the Imperial Court itself. He had simply been in office too long, and those who felt blocked from power, principally Kolowrat, were only too pleased to see the seventy-four-year-old Chancellor relinquish office. For some historians this lack of cohesion within the ruling élite has been regarded as a more pertinent source of breakdown of ruling power than a general dislocation of society ensuing from rapid economic and social change (45). In the case of the Habsburg Empire there is no doubt that Metternich's ability to handle affairs with a singleness of purpose had been steadily impaired from 1835 onwards. From that date he had had to administer the Empire in consultation with the newly appointed Regent, Archduke Ludwig, and the ambitious Kolowrat. Perhaps, then, there is a case for suggesting that the collapse of the government in Vienna was as much the result of the failure of individual personnel as it was the product of social unrest and demands for political reform.

Nevertheless Metternich's resignation and his hasty departure to the town of Feldsberg, 64 kilometres outside Vienna, and his flight across revolutionary Europe to London, represent a major victory for the revolution. It was a conscious break with the past and the Habsburgs were pushed along the path of liberalism, albeit for a short distance. The meeting of the Diet of Lower Austria on 13 March had occasioned demands for administrative reform, the abolition of censorship and ultimately a constitution. By April a constitution had been granted for the German part of the Empire together with Bohemia, Moravia and Galicia. At this stage it appeared that the radical elements of the revolutionaries – mainly the students – were achieving their hopes, and by 17 May the Imperial Court had fled to Innsbruck. The flight of the Court was a further indication of the profound shock and loss of confidence being experienced by the dynasty. This certainly seems to be a feature of other revolutions in central Europe, most noticeably in Prussia, whereas in France by May 1848 the leading bourgeois politicians were already looking to suppress the original revolutionary fervour.

If nationalism was one of the principal causes of the revolutions of 1848 then events in the Habsburg Empire can only be explained by reference to the forces of nationalism. Outside German Austria where national feeling ran high among students, intellectuals, lawyers and some bureaucrats, there was also a stirring among the subject nationalities. The most vigorous challenges to Habsburg domination came from the Italians (see below, pp. 54–57) and the Hungarians. Lajos Kossuth, the foremost spokesman for Hungarian national claims, was an inspiration not only to Hungarians but to Austrian liberals also. In the Hungarian Diet at Pressburg Kossuth's speeches had stoked the fires of liberal sentiment. Most important, the Pressburg Diet passed a series of reforms known as the March Laws, which were both liberal and national in character [doc. 2d]. The March Laws abolished the *robot* and made provision for the election of a parliament on a restricted property franchise. The language of Magyar was to be a requisite qualification for any intending candidate in an election. Effectively this meant that the Hungarians would dominate the Slavic minorities of the eastern part of the Empire as well as a substantial number of Romanians. The whole design of the March Laws would seem to have been an attempt by the Magyar nobility and lesser gentry to substitute themselves for a German-Austrian ruling class. Significantly, although there were some Magyars who were not landowners, there were no non-Magyars who owned any sizeable landholdings (34). This national and economic division was to prove helpful in the later Habsburg repression of the Hungarian revolution.

If Magyar nationalism was sufficiently virile to seek to subdue other racial minorities this was not the case with Czech nationalism, which was the mainspring of the revolution in Prague, in the northern part of the Empire. Like the patriotic movement in Italy the national movement among the Czechs was largely the preserve of an urban intelligentsia. Its leading exponent was Frantisek Palacký, a prominent Czech historian. The height of the Czech movement came in June when a Pan-Slav Congress was held in Prague. Palacký put forward a policy of Austro-Slavism – that the various Slavic minorities, including the Czechs, should be given a degree of autonomy within the Austrian Empire. He took the view that had the Austrian Empire not existed it would have been necessary to invent it in order to protect the Slavic minorities from a predatory Russia [**doc. 2c**]. His programme was not likely to be accepted either by the Monarchy or by those German speakers who lived in Bohemia in significant numbers. (According to Engels there were seventeen Germans to every twenty-four Czechs living in the region of Bohemia.) More to the point, the Germans formed the core of the urban middle class while the Czechs and other Slavic peoples were largely confined to proletarian and peasant occupations. The indications of German dominance were already far too great to allow any form of Slavic independence.

The holding of the Slav Congress in Prague saw the first decisive action by the Habsburgs in carrying out a counter-revolution. A student rising gave the Imperial Governor of Moravia, Windischgrätz, the excuse to bombard the city of Prague. The subduing of the Czech revolution with relative ease and the following victory over the Italians at Custozza did much to revive Habsburg confidence.

In Vienna itself the history of the revolution was much more complex and protracted. The initial victories of the revolution – the fall of Metternich, the flight of the Imperial Court, and the granting of the election of a Constituent Assembly – had been achieved with ease. Thereafter divisions within the revolutionaries themselves ensured the victory of the counter-revolution. From the very beginning there had been a division between the liberal opposition, made up largely of older liberal lawyers and some enlightened bureaucrats, and the more radical democrats made up largely of students (**89**). This division reflected the essential character of the revolution. The liberal opposition wanted to establish the type of régime which the French had overthrown in Paris in February: a parliamentary monarchy. A constitutional monarchy was their ideal. The radical democrats of the Student Academic Legion wanted to go further, possibly to a republic, although they in turn were wary of worker demands. They were in fact content to see a demonstration of workers broken up by the National Guard in August 1848.

The Austrian Constituent Assembly began meeting on 22 July. Foremost in the minds of the deputies would probably have been the news of the June Days uprising in Paris. No doubt they would have been acutely conscious of the danger of the mob and democracy. Consequently the Vienna liberals approached their task with caution. The Constituent Assembly went some way to eliminating the economic hardships of the feudal system against which the peasants had railed. It abolished the *robot* and put an end to the hereditary rights of the aristocracy in local administration. The example of Magyar liberalism and the March Laws was no doubt important. There was no challenge, however, to the power of the monarchy. In fact the Constituent Assembly had been instrumental in inviting the royal family to return to Vienna from their exile in Innsbruck. Just as the monarchy recognised the need to sacrifice Metternich, so the German-speaking liberals of the Austrian Empire recognised the value of the monarchy if the German ascendancy over the Slavic minorities and the Magyars was to be secured. Thus by September 1848 an administration under the leadership of Alexander Bach was preparing to subdue the Hungarians.

The move against the Hungarians demonstrated vividly the split between liberals and democrats. News of plans to send part of the Viennese garrison to assist Jellačić, the governor of Croatia, prompted a demonstration of protest by the student members of the Academic Legion and the Viennese workers. Although there was a small element of mutiny within the garrison, the October Days Uprising, as it has become known, marked the end of the Vienna revolution. Troops under the command of Windischgrätz surrounded the city and a steady bombardment began. Between three and five thousand people were killed (**26**). The October Days Uprising was Vienna's equivalent of Paris's June Days. Both indicated a divergence of ideals, if not always clearly of class divisions, and both marked the defeat of the revolution.

Once Windischgrätz had proclaimed martial law in the city of Vienna the way was open to a complete counter-revolution throughout the Empire. The reaction was implemented by Windischgrätz's brother-in-law, Schwarzenberg, who took command of the Imperial Government on 21 November 1848. The Constituent Assembly in the meantime carried on its deliberations at Kromeriz, but was finally dissolved in March 1849. The rejuvenation of the dynasty had already, in a sense, begun in December 1848 when the feeble-minded Ferdinand had abdicated. Franz Josef, the new Emperor, was imbued with the dynastic ideal and he was in direct accord with the disposition of Schwarzenberg, who wished to revive monarchical and thence bureaucratic authority. Schwarzenberg disregarded the constitutional reforms proposed by the Assembly at Kromeriz. For the time being the Emperor would take command.

The ability to revive dynastic moral authority over the Vienna middle class depended, in part, on the success of the Imperial armies: the Italians were finally defeated on 23 March 1849 at Novarra, only two weeks after Schwarzenberg had dissolved the Assembly at Kromeriz. Any protraction of the war against Hungary might have arrested what amounted to a dramatic dynastic resurgence. It was probably anxiety concerning revival of Habsburg moral ascendancy that convinced Franz Josef and Schwarzenberg of the desirability of accepting Russian assistance to subdue the Magyars. The defeat of the Hungarian uprising was thus finally completed in August 1849.

The liberal phase in the history of the Habsburg monarchy finally spluttered to a halt with the defeat of the Hungarians. Liberal constitutionalism had experienced a short and unsuccessful life. It was easily consumed by more vigorous national rivalries – a desire for Germanic ascendancy over Magyars as well as a Germanic–Magyar ascendancy over Slavs. The willingness of the governor of Croatia, Jellačić, to pit his forces against the Magyars was of the same order as the Gallician peasants' willingness to suppress the uprising of Polish nobles in 1846. Liberalism's timidity and its ultimate defeat is thus perhaps explained: the forces arrayed against it were much too vigorous. Nevertheless economic liberalism did have some success in the abolition of feudal restrictions like the *robot*. But liberal nationalism which had been such a vital force before 1848 was now giving way to a more virulent conservative nationalism in which German hatred of Slavism was the most sinister expression.

9 The German Lands

In discussing the 1848 revolutions it is not possible to talk of 'Germany' in any coherent sense as a nation, as events followed different patterns in individual states. In Bavaria the agitation against Lola Montez pre-dated the news of the Paris revolution of February. News of the revolution in Berlin, the capital of Prussia, came via Vienna. There was a common theme, however, and that was the emergence of a new liberalism. This was as true of the southern German states, like Baden and Bavaria, as it was of the more traditional and reactionary Prussia. In fact it could be said that the acquisition of the Rhineland by Prussia in 1815 was instrumental in dragging Prussia into modern times, because when Frederick William IV capitulated to the revolution in Berlin he appointed Ludolf Camphausen and David Hansemann, two Rhineland businessmen, to head a liberal administration.

It was in the town of Heidelberg in the southern German state of Baden that the clearest statement of liberal aims was made. On 5 March 1848 fifty-one German liberals met in the town and resolved to call a pre-parliament, or *Vorparlament*, which eventually sat on 31 March. Its proceedings lasted until 4 April. The *Vorparlament* resolved that a Constituent Assembly should be elected in order to draw up a German constitution. Of prime importance was the fact that the politicians of the *Vorparlament* believed that the Constituent Assembly should be elected by 'independent' citizens. No doubt the German liberals received reports from Paris and, like their liberal counterparts in Vienna, were mindful of what they would have construed as mob rule: 'It is from Paris that the crowing of the Gallic cock will once more awaken Europe,' wrote Marx (**4**). Some states decided on a residence qualification for those intending to vote in the Assembly elections. In Baden voting was based on a straight property qualification; artisans, journeymen, farm labourers and domestic servants were excluded from the franchise. Elsewhere, those in receipt of charity or public poor relief were disqualified. This was certainly the case in Cologne, where 25,000 people (29 per cent of the population) were in receipt of relief (**81**). So exclusive were the voting qualifications in Cologne and Trier that the labour associations in those towns advocated boycotting the elections altogether as a form of protest. It was hardly a surprise then, when the National Assembly met in Frankfurt in May 1848, that the majority of the representatives were recruited from among the members of the middle class and the gentry. By far the greatest proportion were educated men, with some fifty professors and sixty secondary school teachers, although they were out-numbered by officials and bureaucrats (**81**). Only one peasant and four artisans were elected. The Assembly was in the end nothing more than a reflection of the rise of the official classes: 68 per cent of the deputies were civil servants or officials and only 2.5 per cent were businessmen (**81**). Clearly the care with which the ground rules for the election were designed indicates the wish of the German middle-class politicians to achieve moderate change, and certainly nothing more than the establishment of a constitutional monarchy was desired.

The election of the Frankfurt Assembly was really only an extension of the movement for a more constitutional form of government within the individual states. For instance in Baden the two radical liberals, Friedrich Hecker and Gustav Struve, demanded the separation of Church and State. Hecker was probably more radical than most German liberals, and he did proclaim a short-lived republic at the town of Konstanz in April 1848 (**26**). This was not a very serious threat to the monarchy in Baden and there is very little evidence that there was any fundamental challenge to monarchy as a form of government from the German middle class. Only Ludwig of Bavaria lost his throne and in Prussia it would be fair to say that Frederick William IV created his own difficulties.

In Prussia perhaps the most intriguing feature of the revolution was that the monarchy temporarily appeared to embrace the principles of the revolution. On 18 March Frederick William granted a series of reforms and publicly proclaimed his commitment to German national ideals rather than Prussian monarchical traditions. The actions of the King helped to create the illusion of progress towards German unification, or at least a major constitutional reorganisation of Prussia and perhaps the German *Bund*. However, while the King went with the revolution the Junkers and the army were preparing to crush it. Thus when the Prussian liberals assembled on 22 May to discuss the Prussian constitution the Junkers had already expressed their preferences in the newspaper *Kreuzzeitung* with its motto, 'With God for King and Fatherland'. In the end it was the Junkers who determined the final outcome, but not before the Berlin workers had played a brief but illuminating rôle in events. Berlin's population had grown rapidly in the first half of the nineteeth century from something just over 170,000 in 1800 to a figure over 440,000 by the year of revolution (**14**). The mass of Berlin workers had already discovered on 18 March 1848 that the King had no intention of acquiescing in their demands, although he may have been prepared to meet middle-class requests for reform. On that day a demonstration of workers, largely independent craftsmen, including tailors and shoemakers, was broken up by troops. Some 300 demonstrators were killed. There is a marked similarity here with the events of June in Paris. The most prominent figure to emerge from the Berlin workers' movement was Stephan Born, who had been active in organising workers' committees. Like Louis Blanc in Paris, Born believed that the revolution provided an opportunity for the workers to make social gains, including a ten hour day and the guarantee of a minimum wage (**26**). Again like Blanc, Born did not advocate violence. The Berlin middle class nevertheless viewed him with the utmost fear and suspicion. Both Blanc and Born were unsuccessful, and their failure illustrates the twin themes of growing social tension and the failure of middle-class republicans and constitutionalists to come to terms with the social question. What the middle-class politicians of the assemblies seem to have been concerned with above all was the narrow legal question of constitutionalism or the matter of nationalism.

This preoccupation with the legalities arising from the formation of the Frankfurt Assembly has been the major question for historians (**80**). Consequently the rôle of the artisans in the German revolution has been left to one side. In fact, the artisans constituted a substantial part of the population of most German states and during 1848 they organised demonstrations in a large number of towns including Cologne, Coblenz and Bonn. Very often their attitude was Luddite. They also elected their own assemblies, the two most important meeting in Hamburg and Frankfurt. The overriding concern of the artisan congresses was the growing fear of factory production, the abolition of the guilds and the free movement of labour. They certainly wanted to retain the restrictive practices and privileges of the guild system, but the likelihood of such demands being met by the middle-class Frankfurt liberals was remote (**82**). There was also considerable hostility to Jews within the artisan class in Germany, just as there was among the artisans of Alsace. A revealing example of this anti-Semitism is provided by the handicraft workers of Leipzig: 'There is no greater enemy of the petty bourgeoisie and of the labouring classes, no greater enemy of the solidarity of the small trades than these aliens. . . . Their heart is the money bag' (**82**).

The Industrial Code put forward by the Artisan Congress in Frankfurt was generally opposed to the growth of free enterprise. The Frankfurt *Parlament* on the other hand saw political freedom and economic freedom as inseparable principles. Consequently it rejected the Industrial Code, and in the long run this may help to explain why the artisans welcomed the revival of the monarchy in the German states (82).

The deliberations of the two German assemblies – the one at Frankfurt and the other in Berlin – still have to be considered. The Frankfurt Assembly was concerned with the establishment of a nation state. In all, there were three major solutions put forward. There was a demand from a minority of deputies for the establishment of a German democratic republic. There were those like Heinrich von Gagern who wanted to retain the essentially federal element of the existing *Bund*. This view was supported by the Catholic representatives who were suspicious of anything that smacked of Prussian secularism. Finally there were the Prussian conservatives like von Radowitz, who were more concerned with the integrity of Prussia than with a united Germany. The Frankfurt Assembly was fraught with division and uncertainty not only over the form of government – democratic, republican, federal, secular – but also over the territorial extent of the new Germany. Should it encompass all the German lands including those currently in the Habsburg Empire? Or should it only include those German states that formed the core of the German *Bund*, excluding German Austria?

Not only was there little basis for agreement among the Frankfurt deputies: they did not really possess the power to make their decisions effective. This lack of power was illustrated in the Polish and Schleswig-Holstein questions. Taking the Polish question first it should be remembered that at the Congress of Vienna in 1815 Prussia had obtained the Duchy of Posen. Some Prussian liberals had advocated that Posen should be surrendered in order to facilitate the formation of a Polish state. This was certainly not the view taken by the majority of the Frankfurt liberals, who were more concerned with the 700,000 Germans who lived in the Duchy. The 'temptation' (4) of the German liberals to absorb Posen was too great; it stemmed from long-established assumptions of German cultural superiority in central Europe and, no doubt, a desire to maintain a buffer zone between Germany and the real enemy of liberalism, as they believed, Russia. Effectively therefore, the Frankfurt *Parlament* merely supported the traditional aims of Prussian foreign policy.

In the case of Schleswig-Holstein not only was the ineffectiveness of the Frankfurt Assembly demonstrated but so too was the weakness of Prussia in international affairs. The diplomatic detail of the Schleswig-Holstein question is long and complex but the episode of 1848 displayed the Frankfurt nationalists' dilemma concerning national boundaries. The two duchies had long been claimed by the Danish king, while Prussia had always upheld the claims of the Duke of Augustenburg. The intention of the King of Denmark, Frederick VII, to absorb the two provinces within the Danish kingdom brought a noisy protest from the Frankfurt liberals. They looked to Prussia to defend German speakers in the two duchies. Prussia in fact occupied the two duchies between April and May 1848, but this action brought opposition from both Russia and Britain, who feared an extension of Prussian power into the Baltic and the North Sea respectively. Prussian acceptance of the armistice of Malmö on 26 August and the withdrawal of General Wrangel's troops served two functions. It showed the extent to which Prussia was still the junior member of the alliance which had combined against Napoleon in 1814, and it also demonstrated the fragility of the alliance between the Frankfurt *Parlament* and the Prussian state. The Frankfurt deputies regarded the Prussian withdrawal from Schleswig-Holstein as a treacherous betrayal of the German national cause (80). Prussia's commitment to German nationalism had never been convincing, any more than Frederick William's overtures to liberalism were genuine. Prussia was now to move decisively against the revolution.

In the same month that Prussia had been forced to accept the armistice of Malmö the *Junkerparlament* meeting in Berlin had decided on the necessity of forming a League for King and Country and declared their open opposition to the Berlin National Assembly. By October the King had swung back to a more traditional position and dismissed the liberal ministers. The Berlin Assembly was moved out of the capital to Brandenburg in November, only to be dissolved the following month. The reaction wrought by the new Minister of the Interior, Otto von Manteuffel, marked a revival of monarchical confidence; it also marked the beginning of the end of Prussian liberalism.

Prussia's failure over the Schleswig-Holstein question also had repercussions in Frankfurt. The Assembly had never come to terms with the social problems which had initially activated the workers and brought them on to the streets in March 1848. The workers' demands for a restoration of the guild system, and for compulsory elementary education as well as a progressive income tax, went much too far for the professors and officials of the National Assembly. A popular demand for a refusal to pay income tax in November 1848 was also shunned by the Assembly and displayed the liberals' inability to deal with social questions. This inability had been constant, but now, with the débâcle over Schleswig-Holstein, it had been extended to the national question as well, with the consequence that the Frankfurt liberals became increasingly politically isolated.

The Frankfurt Assembly continued to debate the German Constitution well into 1849, and eventually in March it offered the Crown of a United Germany to Frederick William IV of Prussia. Although not rejecting the Crown outright, the Prussian King claimed that he could not accept the Crown unless it was with 'the voluntary assent of the crowned Princes and the free states'. This equivocal reply signalled the breakup of the Assembly: the Prussian deputies withdrew and the Kings of Bavaria, Württemberg and Saxony would not recognise the Constitution. The plight of the Frankfurt Assembly was now clear. It had no means of enforcing any of its decisions. Its existence had always been at the behest of the King of Prussia and the German princes. The forces of reaction were now irrevocably in the ascendant.

Frederick William's involvement was, however, not at an end. He still believed, with some prompting from the conservative politician von Radowitz, that it was possible to establish some form of unitary German state under Prussian hegemony. To this end a meeting was held at Erfurt, attended by representatives from Prussia, Bavaria, Hanover and Saxony. Although only Bavaria was unwilling to sign the so-called Erfurt Treaty, Frederick William seemed unable to capitalise on the support of Hanover and Saxony. The failure of Frederick William to assert a Prussian claim for leadership of the smaller German states was illustrated by the case of Hesse-Cassel. The Elector of Hesse-Cassel was faced with a recalcitrant local diet that had refused to vote taxation. The Elector withdrew to Frankfurt and appealed to the reconstituted German Diet which Schwarzenberg, the new Austrian Chancellor, had been feverishly attempting to regenerate. The appeal of the Elector of Hesse-Cassel was a golden opportunity for Schwarzenberg to reassert Austrian influence in Germany. Troops were mobilised and the rebellion of the Diet of Hesse-Cassel was swiftly ended.

The case of Hesse-Cassel, like the Schleswig-Holstein question, demonstrates the impotence of Prussia in international affairs and the innate conservatism of Frederick William IV. Thus, if the pendulum had been swinging in favour of Prussia, in terms of leading the smaller German states, during the early 1840s and through 1848, then it was rapidly swinging back in favour of Austria during 1849. By 1850, with the agreements at Olmütz in November, Austria had virtually returned to the situation as it had prevailed in 1815. Prussia was again the junior partner within the *Bund*, despite historical and economic evidence to the contrary. Liberal nationalism was now at an end. It was too weak to wrest power from the monarchs, and instead it elected to place its trust in the unpredictable and prevaricating King of Prussia. Ultimately he betrayed the trust, not in cynical manipulation, but because he was psychologically inclined to defer to Austria, which he regarded as a superior power, and because, quite naturally, he preferred to place his trust in other kings.

10 The Italian Peninsula

A state by state examination of events on the Italian peninsula would be extremely complex. There are three main themes, however, that can be considered in a more simplified approach. First, there was the question of the Austrian presence in the peninsula: Lombardy and Venetia had been part of the Habsburg Empire since 1815. Secondly, there was the general demand for a more liberal and in some instances more democratic form of government, which produced dramatic events in Rome and Venice. Thirdly, there were the grave social and economic difficulties which must have had some impact on the political activity of some of the Italian population.

Dealing with the social and economic difficulties first, Italy is an interesting case, as revolutionary activities pre-date the outbreak of the February Revolution in Paris. There had been more or less continuous disturbances and riots in the port of Livorno from September 1847 onwards (93). This fact may help to reinforce the submission that there were grave social and economic problems pervading the whole of Europe, and therefore that the revolutionary year of 1848 was not a phenomenon explicable in terms of the peoples of Europe following the call of the 'Gallic Cock'. Italy was an economic region of marked contrasts (95), but overall it had not experienced the explosive population growth in the first half of the nineteenth century that was such a distinctive feature of other parts of the continent. Nevertheless it possessed some of the larger cities of Europe. The nine cities of Naples, Milan, Rome, Venice, Palermo, Genoa, Florence, Turin and Bologna accounted for 7 per cent of the total population of the peninsula in 1800 and the situation was very little different by the year of revolution. But despite heavy concentrations of urban population, Italy, of all the regions of Europe with the exception of Russia and the Iberian peninsula, employed a greater proportion of the population on the land than any other area (14). With this heavy dependence on the land there was also, unfortunately, a lack of efficiency.

Italian agriculture was strikingly inefficient (14, 95), and it was particularly vulnerable to foreign competition during the years immediately before 1848. Consequently, there was considerable pressure to transform Italy's basically feudal agricultural system into something that was much more recognisably capitalist. The most extensive changes had probably been wrought in the northern states, in Piedmont, Lombardy and Venetia. But even here the two agricultural systems of feudalism and free enterprise co-existed side by side. For example, in the district of Bologna there were about 45,000 agricultural day-labourers working for wages, but there was about an equal number of peasant landholders or *mezzadri*, who worked a certain number of contractual days on a co-operative basis for local landowners. The vulnerability of Italy's agriculture to foreign competition, its organisational backwardness, together with the heavy dependence of the population on agricultural occupations, meant that natural disasters such as famine were particularly damaging to the peninsula. Vulnerability to foreign competition and organisational backwardness also meant that agricultural products were liable to dramatic price fluctuations. In fact in Italian towns price fluctuations of such a commodity as wheat seem to have been greater than in towns in other parts of Europe. The total price fluctuation in Udine market between 1841 and 1850 was over 59 per cent, and the total price fluctuation of maize was over 58 per cent (**5**), [**doc. 4**]. Naturally enough there had been a number of city riots during the 1840s and these had mounted in their frequency during February and March 1847. There had been outbreaks of Luddism in Rome and demands from the Tuscan peasants for a reduction in the number of labour days (**9**). In the year of revolution itself there were many instances of class-based grievances which resulted in social conflict. For instance, in Livorno, an uprising of workers was put down by a civic guard recruited largely from the local middle class (**20, 2**). The Papal States also experienced outbreaks of worker discontent where there was considerable poverty and unemployment. Count Terenzio Mamiani's liberal government, although wanting to establish public workshops, was unable to fund such a project. Consequently the workers of Rome established a number of radical clubs, demanding higher taxation as a means of eliminating poverty. Just like many of the French and German workers, then, the Italian workers and peasants were motivated by specific economic grievances. These concerns prevailed over more broadly based or generalised political demands such as the establishment of a national state.

Turning now to the question of political demands – the demand for the expulsion of Austria and the demand for a more liberal form of government – which were the other themes of Italian history during 1848 and 1849, it is easy to see that they were the expression of an urban intelligentsia. No doubt there was a feeling among certain sections of the population that the expulsion of Austria would lead automatically to an end of repression and autocracy. In the event, intensification of liberal demands was heralded by a series of progressive acts from an unexpected quarter: the Papacy. Metternich had managed to anticipate most sources of danger to autocracy and conservatism but he must surely be excused for failing to anticipate a liberal Pope. For whatever reasons Pius IX trod the path of liberalism when he succeeded Gregory XVI in 1846, the effects of his actions reverberated throughout the length and breadth of the peninsula. On becoming Pope, Pius granted a political amnesty and encouraged political and social reforms. The press laws were relaxed and a council of state with secular representatives was allowed to share power with the College of Cardinals (**26**). Enthusiasm for reform flourished and other rulers were soon forced to grant constitutional concessions, although Charles Albert of Piedmont, who was ultimately to lead an Italian force against the Austrians, was the last monarch in the peninsula to grant a constitution.

Charles Albert was not disposed to accept liberal reform or any dilution of his personal power. He was, on the other hand, interested in Piedmontese aggrandisement and, unlike Frederick William IV of Prussia, he was prepared ultimately to make war on Austria. Charles Albert's donning of the anti-Austrian cap made him the temporary champion of the patriots, just as the Pope had become the champion of the liberals. The likelihood of war with Austria increased when in July 1847 Austrian troops occupied the town of Ferrara in the north-east of the Papal States. Ostensibly this incursion into papal territory was intended by the Austrian commander, Radetzky, to be a salutary reminder of the effectiveness with which the Austrians had maintained order in the peninsula since the Restoration in 1815. The result was otherwise. The occupation of Ferrara was considered by middle-class patriots and government officials to be a blatant act of aggression. Therefore, just as German liberals had looked to Prussia, so Italian patriots now looked to Piedmont. In the event Charles Albert was to be no more successful than Frederick William IV.

After the heroic 'Five Days Street Fighting' in Milan when the Italian populace succeeded in forcing the Austrian garrison to vacate the city, the stage was set for war. Charles Albert, however, was still reticent, and it was not until after a plebiscite had been held in which the Lombards expressed their willingness to accept Charles Albert's leadership that this enigmatic monarch assembled an army for the purpose of fighting the Austrians. The war turned out to be a disaster. Not only was it a military débâcle, with the Italian troops being defeated first at Custozza in July 1848 and finally at Novarra in February 1849, but it was also politically divisive. The Papacy would not support the war after April 1848 and Ferdinand of Naples, after bringing the Sicilian revolution under control, withdrew his military contribution. In Piedmont the war and the actions of the Papacy caused all kinds of splits and quarrels. Consequently the experiment in constitutional government in Piedmont was far from successful, and there were seven changes of cabinet between 1848 and 1849.

The Papacy's dissociation from the war against Austria was only part of Pius IX's recoil from liberalism. He was faced during 1848 with the demand for even more extensive reforms in the Papal States. Eventually, at the end of 1848, the Pope fled to the southern town of Gaeta, and Mazzini established a short-lived Roman Republic in February 1849. It was to last for three months before it was overthrown by French Republican troops. Cavaignac had already stationed 3,500 troops at Marseille in December 1848 in anticipation that they might be used in Italy but it was not until the Italians were defeated at Novarra that the French President, Louis Napoleon, decided to intervene. If the Napoleonic legend was to be fulfilled, then France would have to overturn the Vienna Settlement and this could only be achieved by checking the Austrians in Italy. French prestige was much more important, then, than the republican ideal of fraternity.

The defence of the Roman Republic has become a heroic episode in Italian history but it did not stop General Oudinot's troops from occupying Rome in July 1849. Clerical authority was restored with a swift vigour by Cardinal Antonelli, though the Pope did not return to the Vatican until April 1850.

The Venetian Republic, inspired by Daniele Manin, fared little better than that of Rome. It eventually submitted to the Austrians in August 1849. After Novarra, Charles Albert abdicated from the throne of Piedmont and shortly afterwards died in Portugal. His successor was able to re-establish royal authority with Austrian assistance. 'The national spirit had vanished,' claimed the patriot Ricasoli (**92**). It is doubtful whether nationalism had affected all the Italian classes. More likely it inspired the nobility and those intellectuals who looked to Italy's past greatness. The lower classes – the peasantry and the urban workers – were motivated by local grievances. For a time they thought that war might solve their troubles, but it was only a short-lived hope.

Part Four: Assessments and Consequences

If a survey for a politicial map of Europe had been carried out in 1845 and then repeated ten years later it would have revealed few differences. Not surprisingly therefore some historians have regarded the 1848 revolutions as failures and have consequently sought explanations for their lack of success. The general conclusion has been that the revolutionaries failed to capitalise on their opportunities. This failure was due, it has been suggested, to the inexperience and idealism of the revolutionaries (80). Related to this general conclusion is the view that the 1848 revolutions in some way arrested or retarded the natural course of history. Evidence for this view is based on the point that within twenty years or so many of the aims of the revolutionaries had been realised: Italy and Germany were united and France became a republic.

To regard the 1848 revolutions as an unfortunate episode in an otherwise uniform march towards liberal government does not help the student who wishes to understand why the revolutions failed. Some historians have attributed failure to diffidence and weakness among the revolutionaries, and this has led them to stress the 'accidental' quality of the revolutions (53). Had the forces of order shown more determination, had Frederick William IV been sane, had not Pius IX been untypical of popes, then events would not have conspired to produce a revolution. The weakness of the forces of order helped to leave a power vacuum in which the revolutionaries paraded with their flags and the liberal lawyers debated until such time as the conservative forces reasserted themselves. There is much in this view since, with the exception of France, Bavaria and the Papal States, the existing governments were not actually deposed. Weakness of the forces of order cannot be explained purely in terms of the frailty of certain individuals. If such an explanation was to be pursued, then the limp acceptance of events by Louis Philippe would be stressed, along with the ageing of Metternich and possibly the arrogance of Lola Montez in Bavaria. Such explanations hinge too much on individuals, and rely on the notion of 'accident'. Nevertheless it could be pointed out that the weakness of individual rulers was mirrored in the revolutionary camp. The revolutions did not produce a politician of inspired genius, leadership, single-minded determination or ruthless cruelty. There were no Robespierres, no Lenins.

All this is unhelpful. A more productive line of examination may be to consider the geographical extent of the revolutions and then to consider the common experiences of that area. One line cf attack may be to ask which countries were *not* affected by the revolutions. It was those countries on the extreme fringes of Europe that were least affected. Britain was unaffected. Admittedly there was a large Chartist demonstration in London, but it was a tame affair compared with the determined violence that had marked the movement in the early 1840s. In the extreme east, Russia was unaffected and even found time to suppress revolutionary activity outside her immediate territory, in the Habsburg lands and Wallachia. In the north the Scandinavian countries were unaffected, and in the south events in Sicily were of an extremely local character. Thus, of the countries least affected, it can be observed that only one, Britain, was very advanced in industrial terms, while another, Russia, was extremely backward – in fact was largely feudal. Within the central area of Europe affected by the revolutions it is probably fair to say that France, Germany, northern Italy, and, to a lesser extent, the Habsburg lands, displayed features of industrial progress and economic backwardness. All these regions were still prone to an agricultural crisis of the traditional type, namely a food shortage. Further, they were becoming prone to a financial crisis of the new type, that is, cycles of commercial and industrial depression. The case of Britain is instructive here because Britain had experienced an industrial depression between 1838 and 1842. The Continent did not experience such a crisis until 1846–47 and this coincided with a food crisis. It was the last time that Europe experienced such a catastrophic food crisis, but it was made all the more serious by a new industrial crisis. Britain's economy, on the other hand, was already on the upturn by 1846.

Given the coincidence of two different types (**16**) of economic crisis it is possible to consider the rôle of different social classes. In France the dissatisfaction of the bourgeoisie with the railway policies of Louis Philippe is clear enough. Elsewhere the determination of the middle class, especially in Germany, to stave off the threat of social revolution from the lower classes, was an indication not only of differing interests but also of the fact that the economic crises of 1846–47 had affected different classes in different ways. As economic privations abated, so any cohesion that the revolutionaries may have had began to disintegrate. This is abundantly clear in central Europe where the peasantry lost interest in the revolution once the more oppressive features of the feudal system had been removed. In the Habsburg lands the peasants seem to have remained passive when Windischgrätz subdued Prague and later besieged Vienna.

In France, the rôle of the peasantry is less clear. Although there is much to be said for the argument that the Second Republic did nothing for the peasants except impose the hated 45 centime tax (**17**), it cannot be said that the French peasantry stood exclusively on the side of conservatism and traditional order as represented by Louis Napoleon. The peasantry were divided and there was considerable peasant resistance to the *coup d'état* of December 1851 (**59, 73**).

Ultimately the most serious social divisions that threatened the fabric of society manifested themselves in the towns and cities. This was clearly demonstrated in Paris in June 1848 and less clearly in Germany and Vienna where no sooner had the middle-class liberals secured the election of their own assemblies than they appeared to be as afraid of revolution as the absolutists. The bourgeois moderates in the Provisional Government in France and the deputies who attended the Frankfurt Assembly wished to be seen as the legitimate heirs of the régimes which they had apparently replaced. This was reflected in Lamartine's obsession with the principles of foreign policy. He hoped to lay the ghost of war and Napoleonic expansion. Similarly it was revealed in the pedantic legalism of the Frankfurt Assembly. The working-class movements and the organisations of the radical left were not, at this time, sufficiently well developed to force social changes in their favour. It is such divisions of interest between the respectable middle class and the tradesmen, craftsmen, artisans and workers that provide the key to the failure of the revolutions. What the revolutions would seem to demonstrate is the fact that when they first broke out the different expectations of the various social and political groups did not really matter. As the course of the revolutions progressed, however, so the different expectations became divisive, and once the cohesion of the revolutionary groups had been impaired the way was open to counter-revolution.

The revolutions failed not just because of social conflicts. They failed because of the policies adopted by Britain and Russia. British and Russian opposition to Prussia's attempted take-over of Schleswig-Holstein helped to discredit Prussia in the eyes of liberal nationalists. Further, Britain's failure to support Italian national claims may ultimately have assisted in the Austrian revival. British diplomacy was directed towards the maintenance of the status quo in Europe, and in this sense Austria was Britain's factotum in continental affairs. Perhaps, too, Britain could not openly support Italian claims for independence because such action would only encourage the subject races of the British Empire including the Irish (**18, 36**). It was ironic, then, that although the success of British middle-class reformers in 1846 had encouraged the Banqueteers and the Dynastic Opposition in France, British diplomacy was still bent on the preservation of order and stability in Europe. This was the paradox of the British position – a socially and politically advanced state, but diplomatically inclined to ally herself with the forces of order and reaction. Russia's position is clearer. Her assistance to Austria in suppressing Magyar nationalism stemmed from an unwavering adherence to the principles of dynasticism and the Holy Alliance.

Following from the reaction against the revolutions there grew up in subsequent decades a more successful form of authoritarian government in France and Prussia than either of those two countries had been able to sustain before 1848. In France Napoleon III was able to achieve a degree of political manipulation and control that was all the more surprising since he allowed universal male suffrage. The use of a democratic franchise for essentially conservative purposes was in its own way revolutionary because, before 1848, those who had advocated universal suffrage had done so in the belief that it would deliver their societies from the whims of monarchs and autocrats. On the other hand, it could be argued that the establishment of universal suffrage was one of the positive gains of the 1848 revolutions. Perhaps Napoleon was watchful of the need to recognise the demands of 1848. The régime made sure though, through the control of the prefecture, that the first parliament of the Second Empire reflected the interests of the Bonapartist cause (**61**). It was not a puppet parliament but it was not designed to cause too many difficulties for the emperor.

In Prussia the resurgence of monarchical power achieved by Bismarck and William I was never seriously challenged. The way in which Bismarck, who was not a modern politician commanding the support of a pressure group or party, flouted the parliamentary constitution of Prussia, created dangerous precedents for German history in the twentieth century. Bismarck was often impatient with parliamentary ways, although he was most solicitous towards monarchs; he was by inclination and training a courtier. Nevertheless, like Louis Napoleon, he recognised the value of the appearance of parliamentary government so long as conservative patronage and control were retained. Both régimes revealed something that must have been quite depressing for the older generations of democrats. The achievement of parliamentary democracy did not radically change society. Indeed, both German and French society successfully retained a marked social hierarchy despite concessions to political democracy.

The continuation of such social hierarchies and the economic inequality on which they were based was a lesson that the mid-nineteenth-century generation of socialists did not forget. In fact, the 1848 revolutions destroyed the idealistic, almost mystical belief that universal suffrage would bring with it social equality. Socialists were already critical of such a political-social equation and they could take some academic satisfaction in the events of June 1848. The 1848 revolutions may have helped to establish a link between the social conscience of intellectuals and the condition of the poorer classes. In the case of socialist intellectuals the 1848 revolutions strengthened their belief that revolution was the scientific and only logical outcome resulting from historical change. For them, revolution was not, as it was to liberals, blind, illogical, destructive violence. Thus the 1848 revolutions provided political violence and conflict with a new intellectual credence and vitality.

If Prussia and France managed to establish a new successful authoritarianism, the same cannot be said of the Habsburg Empire. Admittedly the dynastic ideal had been invested with new life in the person of Franz Joseph, but the revival of the monarchy in the Habsburg Empire was not to prove durable. Ultimately the Habsburgs were forced to accede to the demands for a measure of Hungarian autonomy in 1867. Nevertheless the temporary revival of the monarchy put an end to any liberal notions of a state that united all German-speaking peoples. This may not have been immediately apparent, for in the short run the Habsburg ascendancy over the Hohenzollerns, as demonstrated at Olmütz, would have seemed to suggest the possibility of the continuation of Austrian influence in German affairs. In the long run, however, Prussia triumphed over Austria at Sadowa in 1866, with the result that Austria was banished from German affairs forever. The victory of Prussia at Sadowa was only one event in the political redefinition of central Europe between 1861 and 1866. It meant that Austria was excluded from those two areas – the Italian peninsula and the German states – that had made her so powerful since the Settlement of 1815. Consequently, in a search to recover lost prestige, the Habsburgs turned away from central Europe, seeking compensation instead in the Balkans. Eventually this was to mean a clash with Russia.

If, in those states which could be regarded as traditionally powerful – France, Prussia, Austria – a more successful authoritarian form of government was established, then the Kingdom of Piedmont persevered with constitutional monarchy. Although Charles Albert had reluctantly adopted constitutional ways, his successor, Victor Emmanuel II, was more ready to accept constitutionalism. This enabled the Piedmontese state to accommodate a growing commercial middle class, which in turn was able to harness Piedmont's economic ascendancy to unite the remainder of the peninsula. In this respect the rôle of Piedmont in the unification of Italy was similar to the rôle played by Prussia in Germany. The similarity does not end there, for in many ways Cavour, the Prime Minister of Piedmont after the fall of D'Azeglio, approached the problem of the unification of Italy in the same way that Bismarck tackled the question in Germany. Both recognised the importance of a manipulation of the balance of power in Europe in order to achieve specific national ends.

Cavour realised that Italian unification could only be achieved with outside help. In the event it was French help. Only then could Austria be expelled from the Italian peninsula. From Cavour's point of view this was a military and strategic consideration, for the historian it demonstrates that the causes of the 1848 revolutions are to be found not only in deeply embedded social and economic problems but also in the diplomatic nature of the Settlement of 1815. Given that the statesmen of Vienna had tried to provide a settlement for the whole of Europe, based on the principle of legitimism and denying the aspirations of nationalists, then the 1848 revolutions have an international coherence. Perhaps the liberal nationalists who were active immediately before 1848 had not especially appreciated this fact, with the possible exception of Palacký. Palacký's attempts to restrain Czech nationalism, which was only a strand in a more general Slav nationalism, were derived from a fear of Russian expansion [**doc. 2c**]. In the hands of the post–1848 generation of nationalists, Bismarck and Cavour, nationalism was nothing if it did not manipulate the balance of power.

Perhaps the major political question to deal with is the change in the character of nationalism after 1848. Nationalism did not fade away after the defeats of 1848, but it did change its style. Before 1848 nationalism, beyond the patriotism and xenophobia created in war, was, as a coherent body of ideas, largely the possession of an urban middle-class intelligentsia. They had sought to provide a new and national basis for government that was established by a consent between the people or the nation on the one hand, and the government on the other. Finding justification for their ideas in history, literature and élite culture, these middle-class propagandists had endeavoured to produce rational arguments for a reconstitution of the governments of Europe on national and liberal principles. After 1848 nationalism became an instrument used by conservative politicians to justify the continuation of monarchical power and to promote war. Above all, nationalism proved a powerful force for reconciling the internal class conflicts of the state. Its most skilful exponent was Bismarck who, by a series of patriotic wars, dispossessed the intellectuals of their academic and rational nationalism, making it popular, chauvinistic and aggressive. The nationalism of Bismarck was not the nationalism of Mazzini.

The new nationalism of central Europe represented primarily by German nationalism, and, to a lesser extent, by Italian nationalism, was distinctly illiberal. It was a nationalism that became increasingly racial in character. Admittedly, there had been many instances of xenophobic nationalism before 1848 and there had also been pseudo-scientific claims for the superiority of certain racial groups over others. It was not until after 1848, however, that the scientific arguments became more powerful in their persuasiveness. In 1855 Alfred Gobineau had published his work on the natural inequality of races, and his submissions were given a deeper cutting edge by the apparent conclusions of Darwinian biology. Consequently, although the development was not a simple matter, there arose the view that the only viable form of state was one that was at least linguistically homogeneous if not racially 'pure'. Ultimately the survival of the multinational empires was at stake since any reorganisation of the states of Europe on a national basis seemed scientifically and morally compelling. In terms of practical politics, the new racial nationalism engendered a Germanic hatred of Slavism. An instance of this hatred was seen much later in Bismarck's policy towards the Poles of eastern Prussia during the *kulturkampf* in the 1880s. But, finally, the logic of the new nationalism spelt out the greatest danger to one group – European Jewry.

In international terms the force of nationalism was to redraw the map of Europe. This would not have been immediately apparent to a casual observer living in 1850. It would have seemed that the agreement at Olmütz between Austria and Prussia had effectively revived the Settlement of 1815 and, of course, revived the status of Austria. This was not so. Austria's revival was illusory. The survival of the Habsburg monarchy owed more to individuals – Radetzky, Windischgrätz, Schwarzenberg, Franz Joseph – than to any revitalisation of the system of government. More telling was the fact that the Habsburgs had only managed the defeat of the Hungarians with Russian assistance. Coupled with this, the fact that European governments largely accepted the *coup d'état* of Louis Napoleon in France meant that the Settlement of 1815 had been implicitly rejected (**36**), [**doc. 1a**]. Ultimately this would guarantee the demise of the Habsburg Empire.

The economic consequences of the 1848 revolutions are not easy to tabulate. Economic development is easy enough to discern, since the twenty-year period after the revolutions was a time of unprecedented economic growth and expansion. The early marks of progress which had featured in the British economy were now extended to France and the Central European countries. Even Britain, which had enjoyed sustained growth before 1848, enjoyed even greater economic progress in the years after (**20**). There is a danger, however, of attributing this growth directly to the 1848 revolutions. Obviously the breakdown of old institutional barriers and old customs that had been sanctioned by law facilitated economic growth. For instance, the population growth of Vienna from 444,000 in 1850 to 726,000 in 1880 owed much, no doubt, to the immigration of people from other parts of the Empire. Such migration would not have been possible had it not been for the abolition of feudal restrictions in the year of revolution. In Prussia too, the last vestiges of feudalism were abolished by royal decree in 1850 and all remaining dues were translated into money rents. Large numbers of peasants (640,000) were able in time to purchase their own plots. Modernisation, admittedly under paternal auspices, was one of the stronger trends to emerge in the years after 1848. In Piedmont the level of economic progress was high, and this was fostered by the new liberal consitutional governments of D'Azeglio and Cavour. Even in the Kingdom of the Two Sicilies, which still retained its autocratic monarchy, steps were taken to modernise agriculture and reclaim land (**95**). Perhaps one thing is clear: the régimes that survived the 1848 revolutions were directly aware of the need to modernise their administration, even if they were not prepared to accept a dilution of traditional forms of power.

It should be stressed that the expansion of the European economy and indeed the world economy was due to technological factors, that is causes independent of the revolutionary aftermath. The technical innovations of the railway and the telegraph enabled a broadening of the geographical area over which industrialism could prevail (**14, 20**). Migration facilitated this process. Many Europeans were already on the move before 1848. The movement stemmed from land hunger and a failure of the European agricultural system, which were themselves contributory causes of the revolutionary upheaval. It has been estimated that emigration from Europe had averaged about 40,000 people per annum in the years before 1845, whereas the rate jumped to something over 200,000 per annum after 1848. Much of this movement was made up of Irish, British and Scandinavian migration (**14**). In other words, it was migration from regions that did not play a major political rôle in the revolutionary events of 1848. It would be very difficult to make any precise connections between the revolutionary upheaval and the subsequent rate of European migrations.

What it may be possible to suggest is that the establishment of strong and stable governments in France and Prussia encouraged the growth of industry and trade. Louis Napoleon's ascendancy was accompanied by a rise in stock market prices. Whether one was the cause of the other it is not possible to tell. Nevertheless, in the years after 1852 Louis Napoleon did follow policies that were conducive to economic expansion. The Second Empire has been noted for the emergence of a new breed of dynamic and pushful entrepreneurs, including Pereire, Talabot and Enfantin (**58**).

The expansion and consolidation of industrialism increased the significance of the middle classes. They became, in the stable and more efficient régimes of the post-1848 period, the residual legatees of the *ancien régime*. In Lombardy the breaking up of Church property and the suppression of old feudal privileges strengthened a growing commercial middle class (**95**). Eventually the interest of the Piedmontese and the Lombards converged in favour of unity. In the German states the middle class, which was not as well developed as its counterparts in Britain and France, became increasingly politically conservative. This was probably a direct consequence of the 1848 revolutions. What had happened to an underdeveloped middle class in the German states in 1848 was that no sooner had it made its first excursion into politics than it faced opposition from the German artisan movement. Almost inevitably it became reactionary, never having had the opportunity to be progressive. This had serious implications for Germany's later political development. There is no doubt, however, that the middle classes of Europe made the most significant economic and political gains in the twenty years after 1848. Their ascendancy over other classes was marked, and they were able by the end of the century, in western and central Europe, to reconcile their own economic advantages with the dispossessed classes through various forms of the national-liberal state. Only in Russia did this not prove possible, but in this case the intellectual assertions of Marx's scientific socialism, which had derived so much impetus from the events of 1848, found their practical application.

Part Five: Documents

The politics of conservatism and repression

(a) *After the defeat·of Napoleon in 1815 the Great Powers were determined to preserve the new territorial Settlement of Vienna. This meant that it was necessary to suppress all those 'progressive' ideas that had inspired the French Revolution. The Vienna Settlement was not, then, just a purely territorial arrangement.*

The High Contracting Parties, having engaged in the war which has just terminated, for the purpose of maintaining inviolably the arrangements settled at Paris last year, for the safety and interest of Europe, have judged it advisable to renew the said engagements by the present act, and to confirm them as mutually obligatory . . . particularly those by which Napoleon Bonaparte and his family . . . have been for ever excluded from Supreme Power in France, which exclusion the Contracting Powers bind themselves by the present act to maintain in full vigour, and, should it be necessary, with the whole of their forces. And as the same revolutionary principles which upheld the last criminal usurpation, might again, under other forms, convulse France, and thereby endanger the repose of other States; under these circumstances, the High Contracting Parties solemnly admitting it to be their duty to redouble their watchfulness for the tranquillity and interests of their people, engage, in case so unfortunate an event should again occur, to concert amongst themselves . . . the measures which they may judge necessary to be pursued for the safety of their respective States, and for the general tranquillity of Europe.

The Quadruple Alliance, 20 November 1815, cited in Kertesz (2), p. 13.

(b) *Metternich was the principal defender of the Vienna Settlement and his anxiety about liberal ideas made him particularly suspicious of the educated classes.*

In all four countries [Germany, Spain, Italy and France] the agitated

67

classes are principally composed of wealthy men – real cosmopolitans, securing their personal advantage at the expense of any order of things whatever – paid State officials, men of letters, lawyers, and the individuals charged with the public education.

To those classes may be added that of the falsely ambitious, whose number is never considerable among the lower orders, but is larger in the higher ranks of society.

There is besides scarcely any epoch which does not offer a rallying cry to some particular faction. This cry, since 1815, has been Constitution. But do not let us deceive ourselves: this word, susceptible of great latitude of interpretation, would be but imperfectly understood if we supposed that the factions attached quite the same meaning to it under the different régimes. Such is certainly not the case. In pure monarchies it is qualified by the name of 'national representation'. In countries which have lately been brought under the representative régime it is called 'development', and promises charters and fundamental laws. In the only State which possesses an ancient national representation it takes 'reform' as its object. Everywhere it means change and trouble . . .

We are convinced that society can no longer be saved without strong and vigorous resolutions on the part of the Governments still free in their opinions and actions.

Metternich's Secret Memorandum to Alexander II in December 1820, at the Congress of Troppau, cited in Bridges *et al.* (1), pp. 124–5.

(c) *In practical terms Metternich sought to control the activities within the German universities.*

THE UNIVERSITY LAW

1. The Sovereign shall make choice for each university of an extraordinary commissioner, furnished with suitable instructions and powers, residing in the place where the university is established . . .

    The duty of this commissioner shall be to watch over the most rigorous observation of the laws and disciplinary regulations; to observe carefully the spirit with which the professors are guided in the scientific courses, or in the method of instruction, to give the instruction a salutary direction, suited to the future destiny of the students, and to devote a constant attention to everything which may tend to the maintenance of morality, good order and decency among the youths . . .

2. The Governments of the States members of the confederation reciprocally engage to remove from the universities . . . the professors and other public teachers against whom it may be proved that in departing from their duty, in overstepping the bounds of their duty, in abusing their legitimate influence over the minds of youth, by the propagation of pernicious dogmas, hostile to order and public tranquillity . . .

THE PRESS LAW

1. As long as the present decree shall be in force, no daily paper or pamphlet of less than twenty sheets shall be issued from the press without the previous consent of the public authority.

LAW ESTABLISHING A CENTRAL COMMISSION
OF INVESTIGATION

1. Within fourteen days from the date of this decree, an extraordinary commission of enquiry, appointed by the Diet and composed of seven members, including the president, shall assemble in the city of Mainz . . .

2. The object of this commission is to make careful and detailed enquiries respecting the facts, the origin and the multifarious ramifications of the secret revolutionary activities and demagogic associations, directed against the political constitution and internal repose of the confederation . . .

The Carlsbad Decrees, 20 September 1819, cited in Kertesz (2) pp. 67–9.

(d) *In France conservatism was intimately associated with the Church and the Monarchy. In 1830 Charles X attempted to assert his royal prerogative with the 'Ordinances de St Cloud'. His action precipitated the 1830 Revolution.*

ORDINANCE RELATING TO THE PRESS

1. The liberty of the periodical press is suspended . . .

5. No writing below twenty printed pages shall appear, except with the authority of the Minister of State for the Interior of Paris, and the prefects of the departments . . .

ORDINANCE DISSOLVING THE CHAMBER OF DEPUTIES

1. The Chamber of Deputies is Dissolved.

2. Our Minister Secretary of State of the Interior is charged with the execution of the present ordinance.

ORDINANCE REFORMING THE ELECTORAL LAW

. . . we have recognised the necessity of using the right which belongs to us, to provide by acts emanating from ourselves for the safety of ourselves, for the safety of the state, and for the suppression of every enterprise injurious to the dignity of the Crown.

The main effect of this last ordinance was to reduce the overall size of the electorate.

The 'Ordinances de St Cloud' of Charles X, 25 July 1830, cited in Kertesz (2), pp. 51–2.

(e) *Charles X was succeeded by Louis Philippe, King of the French. Although Louis Philippe was a constitutional monarch, his principal minister, Guizot, who aroused fierce opposition in the 1840s, had firm opinions on the matter of monarchy.*

. . . the throne is not a chair across which a bar has been put lest anyone should use it; it is not there merely to prevent usurpation. Upon this throne is sat a person of intelligence and free will, with ideas of his own. . . . The duty of this royal personage is to govern only in harmony with the other great authorities of state instituted according to the charter; to govern with their approval, their allegiance, their support. The duty of the counsellors of the crown is to win the support of the crown for the ideas, the measures and the policy for which they are sure of support in the chambers. This is what is meant by constitutional government. But to say that the inviolability of the monarch means the nullity of the monarch is strangely to forget the dignity and moral liberty of a human being, even though this human being is set upon a throne and surrounded by counsellors who are responsible for his acts.

Guizot's Memoirs, cited in Woodward (39), p. 145.

documents 2a-f
New political ideas

Liberalism

(a) *The European middle class regarded economic and political freedom as essential to progress. Liberalism included a set of principles that could be used to undermine aristocratic and traditional privileges.*

The Diet has so far not fulfilled the tasks set it by the Act of Confederation in the fields of representation by estates, free trade, communications, navigation, freedom of the press etc; the federal defence regulation provides neither for the arming of the population nor for a uniformly organised federal force. On the contrary the press is harassed by censorship; the discussions of the Diet are enveloped in secrecy. . . . The only expression of the common German interests in existence, the Customs Union, was not created by the Confederation, but negotiated outside its framework, through treaties between individual states; negotiations about a German law on bills of exchange, and about a postal union, are conducted not by the Confederation but by the several governments. . . .

The liberation of the press . . . , open and oral judicial proceedings with juries, separation of the executive and judicial powers, transfer to the courts of the administration of the laws . . . , drafting of a police criminal code, freeing the soil and its tillers from medieval burdens, independence of the communes in the administration of their affairs, reduction of the cost of the standing army and establishment of a national guard etc. were discussed at length, as were the constitutional means that could be used to give force to the just demands of the people. Particular attention was given to possible ways of reducing impoverishment and want and, a closely related topic, of reforming the system of taxation . . .

The Heppenheim Programme of German Liberals, 10 October 1847, cited in Kertesz (2), pp. 79–81.

Nationalism

(b) *Nationalists in the first half of the nineteenth century tended to be liberal in outlook.*

Liberty – Equality – Humanity – Independence – Unity

Section 1

Young Italy is a brotherhood of Italians who believe in a law of Progress and Duty, and are convinced that Italy is destined to become one nation – convinced also that she possesses sufficient strength within herself to become one, and that the ill success of her former efforts is to be attributed not to the weakness, but to the misdirection of the revolutionary elements within her – that the secret of force lies in constancy and unity of effort. They join this association in the firm intent of consecrating both thought and action to the great aim of reconstituting Italy as one independent sovereign nation of free men and equals.

Section 2

By Italy we understand: 1, Continental and peninsular Italy, bounded on the north by the upper circle of the Alps, on the south by the sea, on the west by the mouths of the Varo, and on the east by Trieste; 2, the islands proved Italian by the language of the inhabitants, and destined, under a special administrative organization, to form a part of the Italian political unity.

By the Nation we understand the universality of Italians bound together by a common Pact, and governed by the same laws.

Mazzini's Instructions for the Members of Young Italy, 1831, cited in Kertesz (**2**), p. 173.

(c) *The most vigorous national movements of the first half of the nineteenth century developed in Germany and Italy. Both Germans and Italians could call upon a 'Great Past'. The nationalities of the Habsburg Empire found this more difficult. The timidity of the Czech national movement may be explained by the lack of a 'Great Past'.*

I am a Czech of Slavonic blood, and with all the little I possess and all the little I can do, I have devoted myself for all time to the service of my nation. That nation is a small one, it is true; but from time immemorial it has been a nation of itself and based upon its own strength. Its rulers were from olden times members of the federation of German princes, but the nation never regarded itself as pertaining to the German nation, nor throughout all the centuries was it regarded by others as so pertaining. The whole union of the Czech lands, first with the Holy Roman (German) Empire and then with the German Confederation, was always a mere dynastic tie of which the Czech nation, the Czech estates, scarcely desired to know anything and to which they paid no regard. . . . The whole world is well aware that the German Emperors had never, in virtue of their imperial dignity, the slightest to do with the Czech nation; that they possessed neither legislative, nor judicial, nor executive power either in Bohemia or over the Czechs; that they never had the right to raise troops or any royalties from that country; that Bohemia together with its crown lands was never considered as pertaining to any of the one-time ten German States; that appurtenance to the Reich Supreme Court of Justice never applied to it, and so on: that therefore the entire connection of the Czech lands with the German Reich was regarded, and must be regarded, not as a bond between nation and nation but as one between ruler and ruler. If, however, anyone asks that, over and above this heretofore existing bond between princes, the Czech nation should now unite with the German nation, this is at least a new demand – devoid of any historical and juridical basis, a demand to which I for my person do not feel justified in acceding until I receive an express and authentic mandate for so doing.

The second reason which prevents me from taking part in your deliberations is the fact that, according to all I have so far learned of your aims and intentions as publicly proclaimed, it is your irrevocable desire and purpose to undermine Austria as an independent empire and indeed to make her impossible for all time to come – an empire whose preservation, integrity and consolidation is, and must be, a great and important matter not only for my own nation but also for the whole of Europe, indeed, for humanity and civilisation itself. . . .

You know, gentlemen, what Power it is that holds the entire East of our Continent. You know that this Power, now grown to vast dimensions, increases and expands of itself decade by decade in far greater measure than is possible for the countries of the West. You know that, secure at its own centre against practically every attack, it has become, and has for a long time been, a menace to its neighbours; and that, although it has unhindered access to the North, it is nevertheless, led by natural instinct, always seeking, and will continue to seek, to extend its borders southwards. You know, too, that every further step which it will take forward on this path threatens at an ever accelerated pace to give birth to, and to establish, a *universal monarchy*, that is to say, an infinite and inexpressible evil, a misfortune without measure or bound, such as I, though heart and soul a Slav, would nonetheless profoundly regret from the standpoint of humanity even though that monarchy be proclaimed a Slavonic one. Many persons in Russia name and regard me as an enemy of the Russians, doing me the same injustice as those in Germany who regard me as an enemy of the Germans. I am not, I would declare loudly and publicly, an enemy of the Russians: on the contrary, I observe with pleasure and sympathy every step forward which that great nation makes within its natural borders along the path of civilisation; but with all my fervid love of my own nation I always pay greater respect to the good of humanity and learning than to the national good, and for this reason the bare possibility of a universal Russian monarchy has no more determined opponent or foe than myself – not because that monarchy would be Russian but because it would be universal.

You know that in the South-east of Europe, along the frontiers of the Russian Empire, there live many nations widely differing in origin, in language, in history and morals – Slavs, Wallachians, Magyars and Germans, not to speak of Turks and Albanians – none of whom is sufficiently powerful itself to bid successful defiance to the superior neighbour on the East for all time.

Frantisek Palacký's Letter to the Committee of Fifty of the Frankfurt Parliament, 11 April 1848, cited in Bridges *et al.* (**1**), pp. 136–7.

(**d**) *Magyar nationalism had ambitions to dominate the minorities of Eastern Europe.*

DEMANDS OF THE HUNGARIAN PEOPLE
1 Freedom of the press; abolition of censorship.
2 A responsible ministry with its seat in the capital.
3 An annual parliament in Budapest.
4 Political and religious equality before the law.
5 A national guard.
6 Taxes to be paid by all.
7 Abolition of serfdom.
8 Jury system. Equality of representation.
9 A national bank.
10 The military to take an oath to the constitution; Hungarian soldiers not to be stationed abroad, foreign soldiers to be removed.
11 Political prisoners to be freed.
12 Union with Transylvania.

The speaking of Magyar was to be a qualification for all members of the Parliament.

Demands of the Hungarian People, 15 March 1848, cited in Kertesz (**2**), pp. 125–6.

Socialism – Communism

(**e**) *The variety of opinions subsumed under the heading 'socialism – com-*

munism' is enormous. In the nineteenth century both socialists and communists believed that the democratic principles which had inspired the French Republic of 1792 would never be achieved unless the economic base of society was changed.

COMMUNIST MANIFESTO

1 Abolition of property in land and application of all rents of land to public purposes.
2 A heavy progressive or graduated income tax.
3 Abolition of all right of inheritance.
4 Confiscation of the property of all emigrants and rebels.
5 Centralisation of credit in the hands of the State, by means of a national bank with State capital and an exclusive monopoly.
6 Centralisation of the means of communication and transport in the hands of the State.
7 Extension of factories and instruments of production owned by the State; the bringing into cultivation of waste-lands, and the improvement of the soil generally in accordance with a common plan.
8 Equal liability of all to labour. Establishment of industrial armies, especially for agriculture.
9 Combination of agriculture with manufacturing industries; gradual abolition of the distinction between town and country, by a more equable distribution of the population over the country.
10 Free education for all children in public schools. Abolition of children's factory labour in its present form. Combination of education with industrial production.

Manifesto of the Communist Party, January 1848, cited in Marx and Engels (3), pp. 52–3.

(f) *It would seem that Marx and Engels used the word 'communist' in the Manifesto of 1848 for polemical reasons and to distinguish their revolutionary position from that of other utopian thinkers.*

Nevertheless, when it appeared we could not have called it a *socialist manifesto*. In 1847 two kinds of people were considered Socialists. On the one hand were the adherents of the various Utopian systems, notably the Owenites in England and the Fourierists in France, both of whom at that date had already dwindled into mere sects gradually dying out. On the other, the manifold types of social quacks who wanted to eliminate social abuses through their various universal panaceas and all kinds of patchwork, without hurting capital and profit the least. In both cases, people who stood outside the labour movement and who looked for support rather to the 'educated' classes. The section of the working class, however, which demanded a radical reconstruction of society, convinced that mere political revolutions were not enough, then called itself *Communist*. It was still a rough-hewn, only instinctive, and frequently crude communism.

Engel's Preface to the German edition of 1890, cited in Marx and Engels (3), pp. 33–4.

documents 3a–e
The condition of the workers and the years of crisis

The 1830s and 1840s were years of acute social distress. Middle-class observers became increasingly concerned about the condition of the poor.

(a)
What was horrifying was the sickly pallor of the workers' faces. That second estate could be picked out from those who had remained true to the soil by the fact that its members had, whether near the furnace, in the midst of the iron ore or at the weaving-loom, not only implanted the germ of death in themselves, but had done the same for their children also; the latter, pale and bloated, crept around among the highways and by-ways. Hermann often saw in boldest relief the effect of the two occupations, the one natural, the other artificial, on people. While he saw behind ploughs faces which brimmed over with good health, he was aware of others at machines with sunken cheeks and hollow eyes, whose family likeness enabled one to recognise them as brothers or cousins of the healthy ones.

K. Immerman, *Die Epigonen*, Dusseldorf, 1836, cited in Kuczynski (24), p. 201.

(b)
The second reason for my trip to Germany was that I wanted to engage another good servant. I had had to dismiss my previous one, who meant well but stood around the whole time doing nothing. As the party most concerned, I thought I could put my foot down, but since freedom of trade was universal, I could do nothing about it: any lout could mean well. I wanted to obtain a replacement for my servant only from Germany, for every country has its own special products which one cannot obtain elsewhere in the same excellence.

Spain has its wines, Italy its songs, England its constitution, Russia its Muscovy hides, France has the Revolution and in Germany the servants turn out to be the best.

K. Immerman, *Munchhausen*, Berlin, cited in Kuczynski (**24**), pp. 201–2.

(c)
In this former imperial city one is constantly seeing the influence of traditions handed down from the ancient period of craft guilds, in spite of the French Revolution and the fact that the city had been part of the Kingdom of Bavaria for more than thirty years. It was no longer a question of rebellion and riotous mobs, but attempts were made in those circles which always hoped for a return to the 'good old days' to make life as hard as possible for the new developments outside the Jakobertor [James Gate]. The new developments were that an 'anonymous' company was engaging artisans to put up a building. The question was therefore being asked, how this was to be arranged. The association of journeymen-masons raised an objection that all journeymen-masons or foremen would have to join the association and pay registration fees and subscriptions. The Catholic journeymen demanded additional contributions to the guild's banner, but the masons resisted this; they intended naturally to pay the subscriptions, but registration fees and contributions towards a banner were unreasonable demands to their way of thinking. As they declared that they would rather leave the site than pay these expenses, the situation was made more critical than at first appeared. The magistrate had also threatened the directors with coercive measures if they did not collect the required amount of duty within a week. The manager protested against this, saying that it was not within the duties of a contractor to collect the city taxes. This was admitted by the magistrate, but he pointed out that they had wanted to avoid presenting summonses to individual journeymen and thereby use this roundabout way via the management to pay what was in itself a not very large amount from their own pockets, in order to let the matter drop. Doubtless this solution would have been simpler for the manager, but as he foresaw quite rightly that it might incite people to act in a similar way in the future, he did not take this step. He informed the workers of the demands and had their opposition recorded by the building engineering manager Kraemer in a comprehensive report, which he then sent to the magistrate with the request to have a government decision upon it. The affair was settled when the association of journeymen-masons

was abolished forthwith.

Hundert Jahre Mech. Baumwoll–Spinnerei und Weberei Augsburg, cited in Kuczynski (**24**), pp. 205–6.

(**d**) *Living conditions of workers in Lille*

A succession of islets separated by dark and narrow alleyways; at the other end are small yards called *courettes* which serve as sewers and rubbish-dumps. In every season of the year there is damp. The apartment windows and the cellar doors all open on to these disease-ridden alleyways, and in the background there are pieces of iron railing over cess-pits which are used day and night as public lavatories. The dwellings are ranged round these plague-spots, and people pride themselves on still being able to gain a small income from them. The further the visitor penetrates into these little yards, the more he is surrounded by a strange throng of anaemic, hunchbacked and deformed children with deathly pale livid faces, begging for alms. Most of these wretches are almost naked and even the best-cared-for have rags sticking to them. But these creatures at least breathe fresh air; only in the depths of the cellars can one appreciate the agonies of those who cannot be allowed out on account of their age or the cold weather. For the most part they lie on the bare soil, on wisps of rape-straw, on a rough couch of dried potato-peelings, on sand or on shavings which have been painstakingly collected during the day's work. The pit in which they languish is bare of any fittings; only those who are best-off possess a temperamental stove, a wooden chair and some cooking-utensils. 'I may not be rich,' an old woman told us, pointing to her neighbour lying full-length on the damp cellar floor, 'but I still have my bundle of straw, thank God!' More than three thousand of our fellow-citizens lead this horrifying existence in the Lille cellars.

Adolphe Blanqui, *Les Classes Ouvrières en France pendant l'année 1848*, Paris, 1849, cited in Kuczynski (**24**), pp. 93–4.

(**e**) *It is worth considering whether a distinct proletarian culture and consciousness was emerging in the years before 1848. The development of a 'revolutionary consciousness' has a special place for the historians of the left (**19, 21, 24, 38**).*

... the proletarian is aware of his situation. This is why he is fundamentally different from the pauper, who accepts his fate as a divine

ordinance and demands nothing but alms and an idle life. The proletarian realised straight away that he was in a situation which was
intolerable and unjust; he thought about it and felt a longing for ownership; he wanted to take part in the joys of existence; he refused to
believe that he had to go through life in misery, just because he was
born in misery; moreover he was aware of his strength, as we pointed
out above; he saw how the world trembled before him and this recol-
lection emboldened him; he went so far as to disregard Law and Justice. Hitherto property had been a right: he branded it as robbery.

We too have a proletariat, but not so well developed. If one were to
ask our artisans, who have been ruined by competition and much
else, our weavers who are out of work, silk-weavers, those who live in
our *casematte* and family-homes; if one were bold enough to penetrate
these cabins and hovels; if one spoke to the people and took in their
conditions; one would realise with a shock that we have a proletariat.
Nevertheless, they are not daring enough to voice their demands, for
the German is generally shy and likes to hide his misfortune. But misery grows, and we may be quite sure, even as one day follows another, that the voice of poverty will one day be terribly loud!

Anon., written in Magdeburg, 1884, cited in Kuczynski (**24**), p. 81.

document 4

Bread

*There is no doubt that the poorest sections of the European population spent a
large proportion of their incomes on starch foods. Any fluctuation in the prices of
these staple foods would have serious repercussions.*

STANDARD OF LIVING DATA (PRICES)

Hamburg

(1841 = 100)

	Wheat	Rye	Barley	Oats
1841	100.0	100.0	100.0	100.0
1842	136.4	83.3	98.7	86.4
1843	103.1	83.3	105.2	94.9
1844	109.4	72.7	105.2	101.7
1845	89.5	59.5	113.0	91.5
1846	129.6	91.7	115.6	111.9

1847	151.8	120.8	185.7	149.1
1848	134.0	82.7	124.7	110.2
1849	100.0	53.5	103.9	69.5
1850	100.0	53.5	93.5	72.9

Konigsberg

(1841–2 = 100)

	Wheat	*Rye*
1841–42	100.0	100.0
1843–44	70.9	82.7
1845–46	96.5	131.7
1847–48	108.1	128.8
1849–50	80.8	69.2

Berne

(1847 = 100)

	Wheat	*Rye*	*Barley*
1841		38.5	42.2
1842		42.4	46.4
1843		58.1	61.2
1844		51.5	67.5
1845		49.4	57.8
1846		72.7	71.7
1847	100.0	100.0	100.0
1848	54.5	41.3	47.2
1849	45.8	39.4	42.2
1850	48.4	41.5	45.9

(1846 = 100)

	Bread	*Potatoes*
1836	85.0	
1845	85.0	
1846	100.0	100.0
1847	140.0	136.4
1848	80.0	74.5
1849	75.0	60.9
1850	80.0	65.5

Statistics based on Mulhall (5).

document 5

The secret societies in Paris

Marc Caussidière had been active in the Lyons insurrection of 1834 and had organised secret societies. After the February Revolution in Paris he became Prefect of Police for the capital.

The secret societies had never ceased to exist . . . This freemasonry of devoted men had maintained itself almost unchanged until 1846. Their *ordres de jours* published at Brussels, and often secretly in Paris, sustained their zeal. But the frequency of these proclamations, which sooner or later fell into the hands of the police, made it dangerous to issue them. The relation between the leaders and the other members consequently became limited, when in 1846 a reorganisation of the societies took place, and preparatory steps were taken. Paris was the centre from which the different branches radiated into the provincial towns. These military bodies were all animated by the same sentiment, and were more bent on revolutionary action than on social theories; muskets were oftener spoken of than communism, and the sole formula accepted was the declaration of the Rights of Man of Robespierre. The real strength of the secret societies lay in the working classes, who possessed a certain disciplined force, always ready for action at a moment's notice. They never failed in a single political movement, and they were to be found to the foremost on the barricades in February. In the evening of the 21st February they resolved to proceed on the morrow to the place of meeting, without arms, in small detachments, and to take advantage of circumstances, and, if possible, to make a day of it against royalty.

From Caussidière's Memoirs, cited in Denholm (54), p. 7.

document 6

Conservatism in provincial France

If Paris tended to be revolutionary then perhaps the provinces were conservative.

The nature of the reputation Monsieur Grandet enjoyed in Saumur, its causes and effects, will not be fully grasped by anyone who has not lived for a time, however short, in a country town. Monsieur Grandet, who was still in 1819 called 'honest Grandet' by certain old people, though their number was declining, was in 1789 a master cooper in a very good way of business, who could read, write, and keep accounts. When the French Republic put the confiscated lands of the Church in the district of Saumur up for sale, the cooper, then aged forty, had just married the daughter of a rich timber merchant. With all his own available money and his wife's dowry in hand, a sum amounting to two thousand gold louis, Grandet went to the office of the authority for the district, and there, with the help of his father-in-law who offered two hundred double louis to grease the palm of the rough-hewn Republican who was in charge of the sale of the public estates, he bought for the price of a crust of bread, in a deal legally, if not morally, unassailable, the finest vineyards in the neighbourhood, an old abbey, and some small farms.

As the inhabitants of Saumur were not very revolutionary minded, honest Grandet passed for a daring fellow, a Republican, a patriot, a man interested in advanced ideas, whereas the cooper's interests and ideas were solely concerned with vines.

H. Balzac, *Eugenie Grandet* (1833), Penguin edition, pp. 37–8.

document 7

The influence of the clergy

The elections for the Constituent Assembly in France in April 1848 were the subject of a great conflict between the Republicans and the clergy. The bishops took direct action in trying to influence the election results (60, 63).

INSTRUCTIONS TO PARISH PRIESTS
We remind you of your obligation . . . to urge upon your parishioners the need to fulfil loyally their sacred duty as voters.

We know, dear colleague, the proper confidence they have in you. So help them with your good advice at this important juncture. Teach them how they should both select their candidate and exercise their voting rights. Overcome their objections. Sweep away their fears.

Take pains to explain to them that they are faced with the need to reconcile major interests and must banish all idea of party prejudice. They must concern themselves with one thing only, namely with choosing as their representatives men of recognized integrity who are frankly resolved to set up a Republic in France that respects the sacred rights of religion, liberty, property and the family. . . .

Finally, dearly beloved colleague, set your parishioners a good example. Go to the polls at the head of your congregation.

Instructions from the Bishop of Rennes to his clergy, cited in Price (6), p. 92.

The prelude to June

(**a**) *Alexis de Tocqueville anticipated the events of June 1848.*

In that city there were a hundred thousand armed workmen formed into regiments, without work and dying of hunger. Society was cut in two: those who had nothing united in common envy; those who had anything united in common terror. There were no longer ties of sympathy linking these two great classes, and a struggle was everywhere assumed to be inevitable soon . . .

A dull despair had descended on the oppressed and threatened middle classes, but imperceptibly that despair was turning into courage. I had always thought that there was no hope of gradually and peacefully controlling the impetus of the February Revolution and that it could only be stopped suddenly by a great battle taking place in Paris. . . . What I now saw persuaded me that the battle was not only inevitable but imminent, and that it would be desirable to seize the first opportunity to start it.

Alexis de Tocqueville, *Recollections*, cited in Price (**6**), pp. 96–7.

(**b**) *The Paris police also anticipated violence.*

Excitement and hostility are still at a high pitch in the political groups. The possibility of rebellion is still considered as serious, imminent and inevitable. The clubs have reached no decision about an armed uprising. But the Central Club for the Rights of Man has resolved to use all possible means to summon the people out on to the streets in order to bring pressure on the representatives. It is plain that they have not the confidence to start a battle. But their aim is to organize things in such a way that they will be maltreated by the national guard. Then they will have a good justification for defending themselves – and for attacking in their turn.

Report of the Paris Prefect of Police, 3 May 1848, cited in Price (**6**), p. 97.

(**c**)
I have carefully noted the nature of these gatherings seen in the street over the last fortnight, of the speeches made by the ringleaders, and the fact that the manufacturers can neither get the workers back into

their workshops, where there is employment for them, nor even keep those who had remained. This has led me to the conviction that a hostile organization is behind these disorders. The alliance is organized by the delegates to the Luxembourg.

The delegates to the Luxembourg are represented by an executive committee. Besides this supreme executive council, which represents the combined interest of all the industries, each section has its own committee which arranges for the supreme committee's decrees to be carried out.

Report of the Paris Prefect of Police, 3 June 1848, cited in Price (**6**), p. 100.

June

documents 9a-c

(**a**) *The June Days uprising was provoked by the closing of the National Workshops.*

The total number of barricades of all descriptions in the parts of the city where this reconnaissance took place amounts to two hundred and fifty. Those constructed of planks or barrels are exceptional. Nearly all have foundations made up of paving stones, though the quantity used varies.

. . . Everywhere the paving stones have been dug up and piled on a strip of roadway which has been left intact. The width of the strip varies between 1.5 and 3, 4 or 5 metres. The height is very variable. The widest, which are 3 or 4 metres high, are in the Vielle Rue du Temple and in the Rues Saint-Martin, Aumaire and Rambuteau.

. . . An important feature is the communications system between various roads which the rebels have established across houses, gardens and open land in several parts of the city, especially in the faubourg du Temple. Thus they could, for example, go from one barricade to another in this suburb and in the Rue Fontaine-au-Roi without exposing themselves to the fire of the troops attacking them.

Report of a Military Reconnaissance, cited in Price (**6**), p. 109.

(**b**) *Marx saw the June Days uprising as the climax of a class conflict.*

The Paris workers have been overwhelmed by superior forces; they have not succumbed to them. They have been beaten, but it is their enemies who have been vanquished. The momentary triumph of brutal violence has been purchased with the destruction of all the deceptions and illusions of the February revolution, with the dissolution of the whole of the old republican party, and with the fracturing of the French nation into two nations, the nation of the possessors and the nation of the workers. The tricolor republic now bears only one colour, the colour of the defeated, the colour of blood. It has become the red republic.

There was no republican group of repute on the side of the people. . . . Without leaders, without any means other than the insurrection itself, the people withstood the united bourgeoisie and soldiery longer than any French dynasty, with all its military apparatus, ever withstood a fraction of the bourgeoisie united with the people. In order that the people's last illusion should disappear, in order to allow a complete break with the past, it was necessary for the customary poetic accompaniment of a French rising, the enthusiastic youth of the bourgeoisie, the pupils of the *école polytechnique*, the three-cornered hats, to take the side of the oppressors. The pupils of the Faculty of Medicine had to deny the aid of science to the wounded plebeians, who have committed the unspeakable, infernal crime of hazarding their lives for their own existence for once, instead of for Louis Philippe or M. Marrast.

K. Marx, *Neue Rheinische Zeitung*, cited in Fernbach (**4**), pp. 129–30.

(c) *De Tocqueville also considered that the June Days was a manifestation of class conflict, but he did not regard it as a legitimate conflict.*

In truth it was not a political struggle . . . but a class struggle, a sort of 'Servile War'. It stood in the same relation to the facts of the February Revolution as the theory of socialism stood to its ideas; or rather it sprang naturally from those ideas, as a son from his mother; and one should not see it only as brutal and blind, but as a powerful effort of the workers to escape from the necessities of their condition, which had been depicted to them as an illegitimate depression, and by the sword to open up a road towards that imaginary well-being that had been shown to them in the distance as a right. It was this mixture of greedy desires and false theories that engendered the insurrection and made it so formidable. These poor people had been assured that the goods of the wealthy were in some way the result of a theft committed against themselves. They had been assured that inequalities of fortune were as much opposed to morality and the interests of society as to nature. This obscure and mistaken conception of right, combined with brute force, imparted to it an energy, tenacity and strength it would never have had on its own.

One should note, too, that this terrible insurrection was not the work of a certain number of conspirators, but was the revolt of one whole section of the population against another.

A. de Tocqueville (7), pp. 169–70.

documents 10a–c

Theories of revolution

(a) *The Marxist view.*

The history of all hitherto existing society is the history of class struggles.

Freeman and slave, patrician and plebeian, lord and serf, guild-master and journeyman, in a word, oppressor and oppressed, stood in constant opposition to one another, carried on an uninterrupted, now hidden, now open fight, a fight that each time ended, either in a revolutionary reconstitution of society at large, or in the common ruin of the contending classes. . .

The modern bourgeois society that has sprouted from the ruins of feudal society has not done away with class antagonisms. It has but established new classes, new conditions of oppression, new forms of struggle in place of the old ones.

Our epoch, the epoch of the bourgeoisie, possesses, however, this distinctive feature: it has simplified the class antagonisms. Society as a whole is more and more splitting up into two great hostile camps, into two great classes directly facing each other: Bourgeoisie and Proletariat.

K. Marx and F. Engels, *The Communist Manifesto* (3), pp. 35–6.

(b) *Relative deprivation and revolution.*

Trouble arises if a phase of liberal governmental concessions is followed by a phase of political repression: a phase of fairly open recruitment channels into the élite followed by a phase of aristocratic reaction and a closing of ranks; a phase of weakening status barriers by a phase of a reassertion of privilege . . .

. . . The recipe for revolution is thus the creation of new expecta-

tions by economic improvement and some social- and political reforms, followed by economic recession, governmental reaction, and
aristocratic resurgence, which widen the gap between expectation and
reality.

L. Stone, *The Causes of the English Revolution*, 1529–1642, Routledge,
1972, pp. 16–17.

(c) *Political decay*

If decay is defined as the process by which a set of political organisations and behaviour patterns that have come to have legitimacy and
stability lose these qualities, then the periods just before the European
revolutions can be viewed as times of fairly rapid political breakdown.

J. Gillis (**45**), p. 348,

Chronology of Events

1848

January	12	Revolution in Palermo, Sicily
February	24	Abdication of Louis Philippe
	25	First Proclamation of the Provisional Government in France
	26	Proclamation of the French Second Republic
	27	Establishment of National Workshops
March	5	Meeting of Heidelberg Liberals calls for a *Vorparlament*
	7	Lamartine's Manifesto to Europe
	13	Resignation of Metternich
	14–15	Formulation of the Demands of the Hungarians
	15	Violence breaks out in Berlin
	18	Frederick William IV promises reform
	23	Piedmont declares war against the Habsburgs
April	10	Prussian troops enter Schleswig-Holstein
	23	Election of the Constituent Assembly in France
May	17	Habsburg Imperial Court leaves Vienna for Innsbruck
	18	Meeting of the Frankfurt *Parlament*
June	2	Meeting of the Pan-Slav Congress in Prague
	16	Windischgrätz bombards Prague
	23–26	'June Days' uprising in Paris
July	22	Constituent Assembly meets in Vienna
	23	Radetzky defeats Italians at Custozza
August	26	Prussia accepts the armistice of Malmö, bringing the war over Schleswig-Holstein to an end
September	11	Jellačić begins invasion of Hungary

October	6	'October Days' uprising in Vienna
	31	Military occupation of Vienna by Windischgrätz
November	21	Schwarzenberg becomes Habsburg Chancellor
	24	The Pope leaves Rome
December	2	Emperor Ferdinand abdicates in favour of Franz-Josef
	10	Louis Napoleon elected President of Second Republic in France

1849

February	9	Establishment of Roman Republic by Mazzini
March	7	Schwarzenberg dissolves Austrian Constituent Assembly
	23	Final defeat of Italians at Novarra
April	3	Frederick William IV rejects Frankfurt Assembly's offer of the Crown of a united Germany
June	13	Demonstrations in Paris protesting at French suppression of the Roman Republic
July	3	French troops occupy Rome
August	13	Hungarians surrender

1850

| May | 26 | Prussia establishes Erfurt Union |
| November | 29 | Prussia forced to accept the re-establishment of the German *Diet* by the agreement of Olmütz |

1851

| December | 2 | Louis Napoleon's *coup d'état* overthrows the French Second Republic |

Bibliography

PRIMARY SOURCES

1   Bridges, R. C., Dukes, P., Hargreaves, J. D. and Scott, W., eds, *Nations and Empires: Documents on the history of Europe and on its relations with the world* (Macmillan, 1969)

2   Kertesz, G. A., ed., *Documents in the Political History of the European Continent 1815–1939* (Oxford University Press, 1968)

3   Marx, K. and Engels, F., *Selected Works*, particularly 'The Eighteenth Brumaire of Louis Bonaparte' and 'Class Struggles in France 1848 to 1850' (Lawrence & Wishart, 1968)

4   Marx, K. and Engels, F., *The Revolutions of 1848*, ed. D. Fernbach (Penguin, 1973)

5   Mulhall, M., *A Dictionary of Statistics* (London, 1892)

6   Price, R., ed., *1848 in France* (Thames & Hudson, 1975)

7   de Tocqueville, A., *Recollections*, ed., J. P. Mayer and A. P. Kerr (Macdonald, 1970)

GENERAL BOOKS

8   Abendroth, W., *A Short History of the European Working Class* (New Left Books, 1972)

9   Anderson, M. S., *The Ascendancy of Europe: aspects of European history 1815–1914* (Longman, 1972)

10 Artz, F. B., *Reaction and Revolution 1814–1832* (Harper & Row, 1977)

11 Bury, J. P. T., ed., *The New Cambridge Modern History, Vol. X: The Zenith of European Power: 1830–1870* (Cambridge University Press, 1960)

12 Carr, E. H., *Studies in Revolution* (Macmillan, 1950)

13 Caute, D., *The Left in Europe* (Weidenfeld & Nicolson, 1966)

14 Cipolla, C. M., ed., *The Fontana Economic History of Europe, Vols III and IV* (Fontana-Collins, 1973)

15 Crawley, C. E., ed., *The New Cambridge Modern History, Vol. IX: War and Peace in an Age of Upheaval* (Cambridge University Press, 1965)

16 Droz, J., *Europe Between Revolutions* (Fontana-Collins, 1967)

17 Fasel, G., *Europe in Upheaval: the revolutions of 1848* (Rand McNally, 1970)

18 Fetjö, F., *The Opening of an Era: 1848, an historical symposium* (Allan Wingate, 1948)

19 Foster, J., *Class Struggle and the Industrial Revolution* (Weidenfeld & Nicolson, 1974)

20 Hobsbawm, E. J., *The Age of Capital: Europe from 1848 to 1875* (Weidenfeld & Nicolson, 1976)

21 Hobsbawm, E. J., *The Age of Revolution: Europe 1789 to 1848* (Weidenfeld & Nicolson, 1962)

22 Kranzberg, M., ed., *1848: A Turning Point?* (D. C. Heath, 1959)

23 Kuczynski, J., *Labour Conditions in Western Europe 1820 to 1935* (Lawrence & Wishart, 1937)

24 Kuczynski, J., *The Rise of the Working Class* (Weidenfeld & Nicolson, 1967)

25 Kuczynski, J., *A Short History of Labour Conditions in Germany 1800 to the Present Day* (Lawrence & Wishart, 1945)

26 Langer, W. L., *Political and Social Upheaval 1832–1852* (Harper & Row, 1969)

27 Lichtheim, G., *A Short History of Socialism* (Weidenfeld & Nicolson, 1970)

28 Minogue, K., *Nationalism* (Batsford, 1967)

29 Moraze, C., *The Triumph of the Middle Classes: a study of European values in the nineteenth century* (Weidenfeld & Nicolson, 1966)

30 McLellan, D., *Karl Marx: his life and thought* (Macmillan, 1973)

31 Robertson, P., *Revolutions of 1848: a social history* (Princeton University Press, 1952)

32 Rudé, G., *The Crowd in History* (Wiley, 1966)

33 Stearns, P., *European Society in Upheaval: social history since 1800* (Macmillan, 1967)

34 Stearns, P., *The 1848 Revolutions* (Weidenfeld & Nicolson, 1974)

35 Taylor, A. J. P., *Europe: Grandeur and Decline* (Penguin, 1967)

36 Taylor, A. J. P., *The Struggle for Mastery in Europe 1848–1918* (Oxford University Press, 1954)

37 Thomson, D., *Europe Since Napoleon* (Longman 1962)

38 Thompson, E. P., *The Making of the English Working Class* (Gollancz, 1968)

39 Woodward, E. L., *Three Studies in European Conservatism: Metternich, Guizot and the Catholic Church in the nineteenth century* (Constable, 1929)

40 Wrigley, E. A., *Population and History* (Weidenfeld & Nicolson, 1966)

Bibliography

GENERAL ARTICLES

41   Amman, P., 'The changing outlines of 1848', *American Historical Review*, lxviii, no. 4 (1963) 938–58

42   Amman, P., 'Revolution: a redefinition', *Political Science Quarterly*, lxxvii (1962) 36–52

43   Bergman, M., 'The potato blight in the Netherlands', *International Review of Social History*, xii (1967) 390–431

44   Briggs, A., 'The language of class in the nineteenth century', in A. Briggs and J. Saville, eds, *Essays in Labour History* (Macmillan, 1967)

45   Gillis, J. R., 'Political decay and the European revolutions 1789–1848', *World Politics*, xii (1970) 344–70

46   Harris, D., 'European liberalism in the nineteenth century', *American Historical Review*, lx, no. 3 (1955) 501–26

47   Labrouse, E., '1848–1830–1789: How revolutions are born', in Crouzet, F., Chaloner, W. H. and Stern, W. M., eds, *Essays in European Economic History* (Edward Arnold, 1969)

48   O'Boyle, L., 'The middle classes in western Europe, 1815–1848', *American Historical Review*, lxx, no. 3 (1966) 126–45

49   O'Boyle, L., 'The problem of an excess of educated men in Western Europe 1800–1850', *Journal of Modern History*, xlii, no. 4 (1970) 471–95

50   Tilly, C., 'The changing place of collective violence', in M. Richter, ed., *Essays in Theory and History* (Harvard University Press, 1970)

FRANCE

Books

51   Bury, J. P. T., *France 1814–1940* (Methuen, 1962)

52   Chevalier, L., *Labouring Classes and Dangerous Classes in Paris During the First Half of the Nineteenth Century* (Routledge, 1973)

53   Cobban, A., *A History of Modern France Vol. II* (Penguin, 1961)

54   Denholm, A., *France in Revolution: 1848* (Wiley, 1972)

55   Duveau, G., *1848: The Making of a Revolution* (Routledge, 1967)

56   Howarth, T. E. B., *Citizen King: the life of Louis Philippe King of the French* (Eyre & Spottiswoode, 1961)

57   Lamartine, A., *History of the French Revolution of 1848* (London, 1857)

58 Palmade, G. P., *French Capitalism in the Nineteenth Century* (David and Charles, 1972)

59 Price, R., *The French Second Republic: a social history* (Batsford, 1972)

60 Price, R., ed., *Revolution and Reaction*; see esp. L. H. Lees and C. Tilly, 'The People of June' (Croom Helm, 1975)

61 Zeldin, T., *The Political System of Napoleon III* (Macmillan, 1958)

Articles

62 Amman, P., 'A Journée in the making: May 15, 1848', *Journal of Modern History*, xlii, no. 1 (1970) 42–69

63 Amman, P., 'Prelude to insurrection: the Banquet of the People', *French Historical Studies*, i, no. 4 (1960) 436–40

64 Amman, P., 'Recent writings on the French Second Republic', *Journal of Modern History*, xxxiv, no. 4 (1962) 409–29

65 Baughman, J. J., 'The French Banquet Campaign of 1847–1848', *Journal of Modern History*, xxxi (1959) 1–15

66 Cobban, A., 'Administrative pressure in the election of the French Constituent Assembly, April 1848', *Bulletin of the Institute of Historical Research* (1952) 133–59

67 Cobban, A., 'The influence of the clergy and the "Instituteurs Primaires" in the election of the Constituent Assembly, April 1848', *English Historical Review*, lvii (1942) 334–44

68 Cobban, A., 'The middle classes in France 1815–1848', *French Historical Studies*, v, no. 1 (1967) 41–52

69 Dunham, A. L., 'Unrest in France', *Journal of Economic History*, supplement viii (1948) 74–84

70 Fasel, G., 'The French election of April 23, 1848: suggestions for a revision', *French Historical Studies*, v (1968) 285–98

71 Fasel, G., 'The wrong revolution', *French Historical Studies*, viii, no. 4 (1974)

72 Higgonet, P., Higgonet, T., 'Class, corruption and politics in the French Chamber of Deputies 1846–1848', *French Historical Studies*, v, (1967) 204–24

73 Loubère, L. A., 'The emergence of the extreme left in lower Languedoc, 1848–1851: social and economic factors in politics', *American Historical Review*, lxxiii, no. 4 (1968) 1019–51

74 Merriman, J. M., 'Social conflict in France: the Limoges Revolution of April 27, 1848', *Societus*, iv, no. 1 (1974) 21–38

75 Sewell, W. H., 'Social change and the rise of the working class in Marseille', *Past and Present*, no. 65 (1974) 75–109

Bibliography

76 Stearns, P., 'Patterns of industrial strike activity during the July Monarchy', *American Historical Review*, lxx, no. 2 (1965) 371–95

GERMANY

Books

77 Eyck, F., *The Frankfurt Parliament 1848–49* (Macmillan, 1968)
78 Eyck, F., ed., *The Revolutions of 1848–1849* (Oliver & Boyd, 1972) 1972)
79 Hamerow, T., *Restoration, revolution, reaction: economics and politics in Germany 1815–1871* (Princeton University Press, 1958)
80 Taylor, A. J. P., *The Course of German History* (Hamish Hamilton, 1945)

Articles

81 Hamerow, T., 'The elections to the Frankfurt Parliament', *Journal of Modern History*, xxxiii, no. 1 (1961) 15–32
82 Hamerow, T., 'The German artisan movement 1848–49', *Journal of Central European Affairs*, xxi, (1961) 135–52
83 O'Boyle, L., 'The democratic left in Germany, 1848', *Journal of Modern History*, xxxiii, no. 4 (1961) 374–83
84 Shorter, E., 'Middle-class anxiety in the German revolution of 1848', *Journal of Social History* (1969) 189–215
85 Tilly, R., 'Popular disorders in nineteenth-century Germany', *Journal of Social History* (1970) 1–40

THE HABSBURG EMPIRE

Books

86 Palmer, A., *Metternich: Councillor of Europe* (Weidenfeld & Nicolson, 1972)
87 Rath, R. J., *The Viennese Revolution of 1848* (University of Texas Press, 1957)
88 Taylor, A. J. P., *The Habsburg Monarchy* (Hamish Hamilton, 1948)

Articles

89 Lutz, R. R., 'Fathers and sons in the Vienna revolution of 1848', *Journal of Central European Affairs*, xxii, no. 2 (1962) 161–73

90 Zaceck, J. F., 'Palacký and his history of the Czech nation', *Journal of Central European Affairs*, xxxiii, no. 4 (1964) 412–23

ITALY

Books

91 Mack Smith, D., *Italy: a modern history* (Ann Arbor: University of Michigan, 1969)

92 Mack Smith, D., *Victor Emmanuel, Cavour and the Risorgimento* (Oxford University Press, 1971)

93 Procacci, G., *History of the Italian People* (Weidenfeld & Nicolson, 1970)

94 Whyte, A. J., *The Evolution of Modern Italy* (Oxford University Press, 1944)

Articles

95 Demarco, D., 'L'économie italienne du Nord et du Sud avant l'unité', *Revue d'Histoire Economique et Sociale*, xxxiv (1956) 369–91

Index

INDEX